Over The Other Bridge

More memories from two Leatherhead lads - from the Rising Sun over the Town Bridge to the crossroads

Goff Powell &
Brian Hennegan

Published by

Leatherhead & District Local History Society
64 Church Street
Leatherhead
Surrey KT22 8DP

Leatherhead & District Local History Society is a Registered Charity which was established in 1946 to study the history and natural history of Ashtead, Bookham, Fetcham, Headley, Leatherhead and the surrounding area. It has a library of local history as well as extensive archives of photographs, maps and documents relating to the area.

The Society meets in the evening of the third Friday in the month from September to May at Letherhead Institute at the top of Leatherhead High Street. Lectures are given by visiting speakers and members on various topics relating to the area. Visits are also made to places of special interest.

The Proceedings of the Society are published annually and in addition the Society produces a quarterly Newsletter containing details of activities as well as articles written by members about their particular areas of interest. Publication is an essential part of the Society's activities and, from time to time, books and pamphlets are published concerning the history of our local area.

The Society owns and manages Leatherhead Museum which is housed in Hampton Cottage in Church Street and was opened in 1980. We are an Accredited Museum with a varied collection of artefacts relating to the area.

ISBN 978-0-9572408-2-7

CONTENTS

Introduction

Acknowledgements

Chapter 1   The 'Rising Sun' to the River Mole   1

Chapter 2   A Sporting and Energetic Interlude   15

Chapter 3   The Town Bridge and Mill   23

Chapter 4   The Foot of the Bridge - On the Town Side   29

Chapter 5   Our Journey up Bridge Street - Along   33
             the Northern Side

Chapter 6   The South Side from Minchin Close   50
             to the Crossroads

Bibliography   67

INTRODUCTION

In 2009 The Leatherhead & District History Society published a book by Brian Hennegan entitled 'Over the Bridge'. This was followed in 2011 by another one called 'Over the Bridge the Southern Side', by Brian Hennegan and Goff Powell.

Both authors felt that it would be fitting to write another book about Leatherhead, thereby completing a 'Bridge Trilogy'. The two previous books had featured the Kingston Road railway bridge in their title.

This third book still follows 'The Bridge' theme but this time the bridge in question is the Town Bridge, over the River Mole, at the foot of Bridge Street.

When we first thought about the format that the book should take we had intended to cover all streets in the town, with the exception of North Street. (A journey along both sides of North Street can be made by reading 'Over the Bridge the Southern Side' by the same authors and published by The Leatherhead & District Local History Society).

However we very soon realized the format would produce a book that would be too large. Therefore in the offering we put before you, dear reader, we will begin at the site of 'The Rising Sun' public house (at the junction of Cobham Road and Hawks Hill) and travel up Bridge Street, ending our journey at the crossroads in the Town Centre. Yes, we are aware that the 'Rising Sun' site is in Fetcham, but it does allow us to 'cross over the bridge' and visit some interesting places en-route.

In any project such as this you have to decide how far back in time one should travel. At some locations the 'historical thread' will extend further back than at others. However at most sites we will be exploring into the nineteenth century and possibly beyond.

It is sometimes difficult to remember what changes have taken place before the latest development appeared, even though we have witnessed the transition. Both of the authors have lived in Leatherhead for more than seventy years thus enabling them to intersperse their personal recollections with historic fact.

Although some places have changed beyond all recognition it is gratifying to see how many of the 'old land marks' are still with us. The question is for how long? As a prime example, in our recent book 'Over the Bridge the Southern Side' we waxed lyrical over the Police Station in Kingston Road. Alas at the time these words are being written it is no more, having sacrificed its space for residential accommodation.

Our journey will take us, from the river, up the Northern Side of Bridge Street. We will then walk back down to the river and journey back up the Southern Side. To avoid confusion the left hand side, as we walk up Bridge Street, will be referred to as the 'Northern Side'. Likewise the right hand side as we walk up will be referred to as the 'Southern Side'.

The authors hope that they have been reasonably successful in weaving a path through the years and that the finished offering will provide the reader with an enjoyable glimpse into the past and resurrect many latent memories.

ACKNOWLEDGEMENTS

It would not be possible to have written this book without the help and advice of a number of people. Also the permission to quote freely from previous books and articles, many of which were written by fellow members of The Leatherhead & District Local History Society, both past and present, has been invaluable.

A list of bibliography appears at the end.

As always, it is dangerous to name individuals for fear of omitting some. However we would like to place on record the help and advice we received from our good friend Alun Roberts. He was able to fill in some of the gaps concerning Benjamin Simmons, who was around in the 18th century and left 'his footprint' on the Town. He also offered words of advice, which we were glad to take on board.

Edwina Vardey and the late Linda Heath had previously said that we could always use information from their books. Without recourse to these admirable facilities there might have been some areas of 'daylight' in this current offering.

Readers of our book 'Over the Bridge the Southern Side', will have seen that we recorded our thanks to Mrs Joy Playford and once again she was able to clarify the confusion surrounding the various names of Emlyn Lane.

Other people that have assisted us with specific information are mentioned in the text. However if we have failed to mention by name those to whom we have spoken, especially whilst we have been performing our duties at The Leatherhead Museum, you know who you are, so please accept our thanks.

As with the previous books this one will contain some photographs which might not have been seen before. Many of these pictures come from the extensive photo library that has been compiled by Goff Powell over many years. Other pictures are from the collection of The Leatherhead & District Local History Society or friends.

Last of all, but by no means least, we give our sincere thanks to our good friend and fellow Society member Martin Warwick. Without his considerable help and input the following would have consisted of a random selection of text and pictures, the juxtaposition of which would have left a lot to be desired.

Chapter 1

THE 'RISING SUN' TO THE RIVER MOLE

Our journey starts at the junction of Cobham Road and the Guildford Road, just at the foot of Hawks Hill. For many years a stranger seeking directions in the area would have heard the words "you go left, right or straight on at The Rising Sun." This local tavern had dominated the area for many years. There were in fact two such hostelries. The original 'Rising Sun' is currently a Chinese restaurant called 'Zen Garden'.

What a tranquil scene. In this c1920 view we are looking towards the Railway Bridge. The impressive name-board along the eaves makes it clear that Hodgson's are in residence.

Whilst we are here let us linger a while and take a closer look at the 'Old Rising Sun' building. For many years a statement on the wall of the building proclaimed in 'Olde English' a date of c1348. There is a theory that the building was once a priest's house. In 1528 it was called Chapel House. A 'Chapel', dedicated to Saint Katherine was situated in close proximity and is referred to in a deed of that date. The building was originally an open 'hall-type' house that went from the floor right up to the roof timbers but it was later converted to a two storey house. Further changes and additions were probably made in the early 19th century and in more recent times.

At one time it was probably an ale house that at some indeterminable date became known as 'The Rising Sun'. In the late 18th century Thomas Cooper was the landlord and he began a successful business 'brewing six-penny beer from fine spring water'. The many springs adjacent to the Mill Pond ensured a steady supply of this important ingredient. Thomas Cooper went on to found 'The Lion Brewery' in North Street, not to be confused with 'The Swan Brewery' in the High Street. Thomas died in 1799 by which time he owned 80 public houses in the district. Not surprisingly, he lies under the grandest tombstone in Leatherhead Churchyard.

In 1805, at the same time that Admiral Lord Nelson was engaged in a fracas with the French, 'The Rising Sun' was described as 'A compact brew house, storeroom and cellar capable of holding 78 butts of beer, i.e. 8,424 gallons'. Hodgson's Brewery, of Kingston, purchased the premises in 1896.

During the Second World War the establishment was used as a Youth Hostel.
Here we see a group of happy 'inmates' circa mid-1940s.

For a short while it was called 'Perquins Restaurant' and during the Second World War it was used as a youth hostel. Following that it became 'Ye Olde Rising Sun'. Both your authors knew and visited the establishment and one of them had his wedding reception there over fifty-three years ago.

This evocative sketch was made in the 1950s. It is easy to imagine sitting here in days long ago, feeling the warmth from the open fire, hearing the chatter of voices and the rattle of dominoes on the table.

It remained a public house until the new 'Rising Sun' was opened, on the opposite corner of the road junction, in the late 1930s. Over the years the establishment has been known by a number of names; 'The Pilgrims Rest', 'Le Pelerin', 'Pangs-Villa', 'China Red' and currently (2015) 'Zen Garden'. In Thomas Cooper's day China was one of those 'faraway places with strange sounding names', now it seems we are all dining on Chinese Cuisine. There is still a small brick built structure behind the

It is surprising how quickly our memories fade.
The new building in all its glory, circa early 1960s.

original building, that for many years was home to a forge, reminding us of the important part played by 'horse power' in those days of yore.

The 'new' Rising Sun was built by Hodgson's Brewery of Kingston, in the 'modern architectural style' that they adopted for corner sites. Further examples of this style can be seen at The Bell, Fetcham and The Crown, Bookham. Although they differ to suit their site, many architectural features are common to all of the buildings.

Tally Ho! "Fill the Stirrup Cup Charles." The hunt, all 'suited and booted' preparing for a
scintillating gallop over the Downs.
The picture is taken in front of the 'new' Rising Sun, c1940.

The 'new' Rising Sun was another popular venue for a 'Meet'. This photograph must have been taken soon after the beginning of the Second World War before the threat of invasion prompted the removal of signposts. The Old Rising Sun can be seen in the background. Also noticeable, running across the photograph, is the railway embankment bereft of trees, as was the practice of the day. There were no 'leaves on the line'.

For many years the pub was a well-known stop-off for coaches returning to London after a day out at the seaside. The establishment even supplied its own piano player, shades of Mrs. Mills. If we concentrate we might be able to hear the enthusiastic harmonies of all those pre and post war songs. Please make sure that you sing the 'proper' words. The Courage Group eventually purchased the Hodgson Brewery and 'The Riser' changed hands. In recent years it became part of the Harvester chain of restaurants. This well-known land mark was demolished in 2005 and apartments were built on the site.

This is a recent view of Harrow Way Manor that now occupies the site of the 'new' Rising Sun. The pub was demolished in 2005.

Just before we leave the junction take a look at the wall on the opposite side of the Guildford Road. In times gone by it was taller than now and in the 1930s the 'phantom painter' had struck and painted the words 'Strike Now in The West' so that it was clearly seen by those folk coming along Cobham Road. Those of you who have read the authors' book 'Over the Bridge the Southern Side' will find further references to this phantom painter. To what did this rampant vandalism refer?

We now make our way along the road in the direction of the railway bridge. Just past 'Ye Olde Rising Sun' building, now called Zen Garden, we come to the row of shops called Sunmead Parade, aptly named after Sunmead House that had previously occupied the site. It was demolished around 1935 and was described as a regency house that had been revamped with the addition of a Georgian front. Maps confirm that it was built in 1791 in the 'Sun Mead', which belonged to The Rising Sun next door.

At the same time, c1935, the small 'cul-de-sac' off the Cobham Road, called Sunmead Close, was built and a footpath running beside the row of shops was retained.

Sunmead house before it was demolished c1935 to make way for Sunmead Close and the parade of shops.

The 1940 Kelly's Street Directory lists the following shop occupants, commencing at the Railway Bridge end; No. 1 Clark's Café, No. 2 Invincible Policies Ltd, No. 3 J. Peachy News Agent. By the 1950s Invincible Policies Ltd had relocated in the High Street and The Ministry of Labour and National Service Employment Exchange had moved from Cannon Grove Fetcham into No. 2 Sunmead Parade.

This is a recent picture of Sunmead Parade. On the end wall the notice proclaims 'Clark's Café Established 1935'. The Labour Exchange, to give it its popular name, was located in the centre shop, now Domino's Pizzas.

There must be many men still living in the area who can recall having to enlist for National Service at these premises. One of your authors joined this pilgrimage, took 'The Queen's Shilling' (or to be more correct, he had 'The Queen's Shilling' thrust upon him) and commenced two years of 'encouragement and enlightenment'.

In the early days the News Agents changed hands several times before the Edwards family occupied it for a long period; it is now Nikki News, Groceries and Convenience Store. No. 2 was unoccupied for some time and is now Domino's Pizzas. Although it has changed ownership on a number of occasions the name Clark's Café remains. The sign on the side of the building tells us that Clark's Café was established in 1935.

The land between Sunmead Parade and the railway line is now occupied by a recently developed office complex. Prior to April 1999 the whole area was home to Leatherhead Bus Garage which was opened by East Surrey Traction Company on 1st June 1925. The original garage consisted of three sheds built close up to the railway embankment with the entrances facing on to the Guildford Road. It soon became evident that the accommodation was not sufficient and just prior to the Second World War the garage was extended on land that had been previously purchased, taking the garage boundary right up to the wall of Clark's Café. (Incidentally during the years that the garage was open the café had a steady flow of customers provided by the bus crews and garage personnel).

What a fine collection of vehicles. They belong to the East Surrey Traction Company. The Company name can be seen along the roof girder, behind the buses. Date of the photograph is early 1930s.

By the time the garage was extended London Transport had taken over the operation of buses in the London 'central' and 'country' areas. The additional buildings constructed in the London Transport house style were modern and easy on the eye. Similar design features could be seen on London Transport garages in many places e.g. Dorking, Godstone, Windsor and St Albans, just to name a few. By the mid-1950s the garage was responsible for operating and servicing a large number of vehicles, so it was decided to extend upwards and the second floor became home to a staff canteen and additional offices. As an example of how the requirements had increased, in June 1938 the garage housed and serviced 27 buses and 7 coaches. In October it was responsible for 59 buses.

One of your authors has memories of war time travel when experiments were made with gas powered vehicles. The system required the bus to tow a small two wheeled unit known as a 'gas producer' which burnt anthracite, this formed a gas which was then fed to the engine. This system was only successful on fairly flat routes and the 462 route to Staines seemed a likely candidate. He travelled on 'the swinger' to School in Fetcham. A fuel store for this system was built in the garage yard and it remained in situ for many years after the war had ended.

We include this picture because it serves two purposes, namely to show the enlarged Bus Garage and the effect of the devastating 1968 floods. In fact by the time this photo was taken the waters had receded below the tops of the cars.

Perhaps it is worth reminding ourselves that the local company of Neil and Spencer Limited played a part in the development of this form of vehicle power. During the war they were based in premises at Effingham Crossroads and two London Transport 'STL' type double deck buses were registered to them. After the war the company moved to premises in Station Road.

As the years passed travel habits changed and bus companies had to revise both their route patterns

A 462 bus towing a gas producer trailer, during the Second World War.

and frequency of service. This resulted in the closure of the garage on 30th April 1999. The buildings were demolished very quickly after that and the existing office buildings were erected. The Leatherhead Bus Garage had served the community effectively for almost 75 years.

7

This c1970 photo shows the upper story that was added in the early 1960s. It housed the canteen and offices. The architectural style of the ground floor was common to all the London Transport garages built in the 1930s and examples could be seen at Dorking, St. Albans, Windsor to name a few. The 'sheds' in the background are the original East Surrey buildings and remained in situ until the end.

We will now make our way under the railway bridge that carries the line on to Dorking. It was originally constructed by 'The London Brighton and South Coast Railway' and trains first ran over the line on 11th March 1867. As we come under the railway bridge we are confronted by one of those 'marmite' buildings, which you either like or loathe, it is of course the Water Pumping Station.

The legend on the top of the building proudly proclaims 'East Surrey Water Company. Leatherhead

Building on the grand scale - nobody could say that The East Surrey Water Company was bashful!

Pumping Station New Works 1935'. The building was doubled in size in 1940 and this date is shown on the other end of the complex. The building is an imposing structure built in concrete using the slip forming method. The distinct lines showing the 'strata' can be clearly seen on its walls. The pumps, fed by four bore holes, were originally diesel powered but in 1984 electric pumps were installed. The tanks containing the diesel fuel were located between the pump house and the River Mole. One of these tanks can just be seen below. During the war, these tanks were hit by an incendiary bomb and all hell was let loose.

One of the tanks mentioned can be seen on the left hand side of the picture

Were the roads really this deserted? Well they seemed to be in the late 1950s. The Green London Transport RT bus is on the 418 route to Bookham. In the centre background the Green Domino Hotel looms large.

We have now arrived at the Western end of the Town Bridge that spans the River Mole, but we are not going to cross over it just yet. We will look at this venerable structure in some detail in a later chapter. Instead we will cross over the road, please be careful, and investigate the changes that have taken place over the years between here and the Railway Bridge. The new offices, at the entrance to the Leisure Centre, now occupy a site that was very different even just a few years ago.

In the last years of Queen Victoria's reign some of the larger houses in the area, for example Cherkley Court and The Red House, had their own generating equipment which was admired by many. On the 8th July 1899 a provisional order for electric lighting was made, but it was not immediately put into action. In 1902 the Town Council agreed to its adoption and the local firm of Buchanan and Curwen were engaged to carry out the installation in a number of roads, including Copthorne Road, Woodvill Road, Kingston Avenue, Clinton Road, and Reigate Road.

The offices and showrooms of the Leatherhead & District Electricity Company circa early 1900s.
They would be demolished in 1934 to make way for the New Pumping Station.
The Town Bridge is out of shot to the right.

In 1925 the Leatherhead & District Electricity Company Ltd (later the London and Home Counties Joint Electricity Authority and eventually Seeboard, established a new works and substation on the West bank of the river along with three houses called 'Electricity Cottages'. By 1941 the works had been shut down as the town was fed by bulk supplies from the National Grid. The cottages have now been demolished and replaced by more modern homes but a small substation still remains.

ELECTRICITY

is supplied in

ASHTEAD, LEATHERHEAD & MICKLEHAM

BY

THE LEATHERHEAD AND DISTRICT ELECTRICITY Co., Ltd.

One of the four Generators in th Bridge Street Power-House.

GAS IS NOW TOO DEAR!

Write us for full particulars of our FREE WIRING scheme, which enables you to have a dainty and complete electric light installation FREE of any initial outlay.

HEATING APPARATUS AND MOTORS ON HIRE

LOW RATES FOR POWER AND HEATING

One of the four generators –
Bridge Street 1910.

Entrance to Fetcham Grove House in 1910. The Electricity
Company offices can be seen on the left of the picture.

The photograph shows the high wall and entrance to Fetcham Grove House in 1910. It must have been quite a splendid structure in its time. Shortly after this the building was unoccupied. We believe the wall was demolished around the 1920s, when the main house became the Green Domino Hotel. In Later years the well-known removal company called 'Bishop's Move' had their offices there and the bright yellow vans, sporting the Red Bishop chess piece, could be seen parked in front of the building. Although part of the high wall did remain in front of the West Wing of the house, it was pulled down along with the main building in 1998. We will pay another visit to this building in the next chapter.

Once a familiar sight in and around the town. This is one of Bishop & Sons distinctive bright yellow pantechnicans, sporting their famous Red Bishop chess piece.

Many local people will remember Bridge Motors Garage on the Guildford Road, between the Electricity Station and The Green Domino. Just when the garage was established is not known, but a 1936 Street Directory tells us it was known as Bridge Motors (C.J. Fry) Motor Engineers. In 1940 the owner was George White. Like many garages during the Second World War they produced parts for the war effort. In 1945 it became a Limited Company. The garage remained in the White family until the late 1980s.

The garage has been replaced by an office block originally called Riverside Court and following a refurbishment, Grove House and yet more offices. Riverbridge House has been built on what remained of the old 'Seeboard' works.

BRIDGE MOTORS
(LEATHERHEAD) LTD.
MOTOR AND GENERAL ENGINEERS

Agents for
all Leading Makes of Cars and Insurance Companies

CAR OR VAN LOAN SERVICE—
WHILST YOURS IS UNDER REPAIR

Complete Overhauls and Repairs, including Re-Boring
CELLULOSE SPRAYING AND COACHWORK REPAIRS
Special Machine-Work undertaken　　:　　Tecalemit Servicing Process
GUILDFORD RD., LEATHERHEAD
Tel.: Leatherhead 2564　　　　Car Hire Service

Bridge Motors Advert circa late 1950s. Note the four digit telephone number!

In September 1968 the River Mole burst its banks. On the 14th there had been almost continuous rain, but on the 15th 4.62 inches fell in six hours and by the evening the water had risen to a new

Road junction of Waterway Road and Guildford Road circa early 1960s and after the time of the accident. Note the advertising hoardings and the lack of vegetation on the railway embankment.

recorded level. The resultant floods inundated the Bus Garage, the Fire Station and Bridge Motors, properties on the town side of the bridge and many acres of countryside. The Leatherhead Council told The Leatherhead Advertiser "About 1,072 million gallons of water poured through the town during the worst of the floods, engulfing homes and disrupting traffic in two days of disaster."

Before we leave this area it might be of interest to take a look at the road layout where Waterway Road leaves the Guildford Road. Around sixty five years or so ago, the 'triangular roundabout' did

View of the old Waterway Road Bridge from 1965. Note the '4 SUB' train, which would be painted in the BR Southern region Green. Beyond we see the two Railway Bridges. The first one is rather ornate and was built by The London, Brighton and South Coast Railway. The one in the far distance was built by the London and South Western Railway.

not exist and there was a 'T' junction close to the front of the Pumping Station (being a continuation of Mill Lane). One of the authors was coming out of Waterway Road with a friend, riding bikes (of the pedal variety) and the friend collided with a car. Fortunately no great harm was done to him, but his bike was somewhat 'modified'.

In the introduction we said that on occasion we might deviate from the original plan. Well now is the time for one of those deviations. Come with us a little way along Waterway Road as far as the bridge. The two photographs of this location will be of interest and the captions will speak for themselves.

The new Waterway Road Bridge under construction in 1980 to make ready for the new traffic flow system. Part of the original Pumping Station can be seen in the centre background.

The original road bridge was erected in the days when road traffic was light, both in weight and frequency; however after the Second World War this situation began to change dramatically. When the 'new' one-way traffic system was created the road over the bridge became a main traffic artery.

In 1980 it was decided, not before time, to rebuild the Waterway Road Bridge. Whilst this was taking place the traffic was kept moving, using a temporary single lane 'Bailey Bridge' that was controlled by lights.

The original Water Pumping House complete with its chimney dating from 1884, stood on the West bank of the river, on the up-stream side of the road. This, together with the adjacent water tank, was demolished in 1992 to make way for the apartments now occupying the site.

Another small, late Victorian building relating to the Water Works, still stands on the opposite bank of the river. It originally housed pumps for a sewerage control system. In later years the building was used by The Leatherhead and District Scout Association for storing canoes.

This delightful building still stands, a little bit of Victorian architecture surrounded on all sides by modernity. There is a screen of trees now covering its river aspect. Perhaps it no longer wishes to gaze upon the modern world.

View from the Bridge looking towards Waterway Road c1930s with the Sewer Pump House on the right hidden by the trees.

Before the trees grew.

Whilst we are still on the Western side of the river we felt we could not leave until we had taken a look at the area known as Fetcham Grove. It is here that some of our fellow townsfolk and those from further afield, engage in various forms of physical activity, so we decided that a whole chapter should be devoted to it and hope that you are energetic enough to join us.

Chapter 2
A SPORTING AND ENERGETIC INTERLUDE

Fetcham Grove House c1930s showing the additional West Wing on the right hand side.

Why is it called Fetcham Grove you may ask? It is named after Fetcham Grove House that stood just West of the Leatherhead Bridge. Robert Sherson, an antiquary and apothecary, bought the house in about 1788. For over 35 years it was occupied by the Clagett family and for a further 20 years by the wine merchant Ernest Secretan. About 1882 it was bought by the grandly named General Henry de Tessier (later Baron) of the Royal Artillery.

The original house was described in the 1780s as a 'square brick house'. Later various extensions were added, especially the adjoining 'West Wing'. In the 1920s the house and grounds were the property of Herbert K. Reeves the well-known local benefactor. For many years Fetcham Grove was either known as The Green Domino Café or Green Domino Hotel & Restaurant. A 1930s advert for West Wing offers the following:- Swimming Pool, Hard Tennis Courts, Grass Court and a Squash Court. Tuition in all subjects; Moderate Prices & Season Tickets, adjoining Restaurant.

West Wing Swimming Pool. Much missed on a very hot summer's day.

You may recall us mentioning the West Wing Swimming Pool in 'Over The Bridge the Southern Side', alas it closed with the coming of the Leisure Centre in the early 1970s leaving many townsfolk with happy memories of stretching out on the grass after a cooling dip in the pool. Both of your authors remember gaining one of their scout badges by swimming one mile. They think they had to do 70 or 72 lengths and recall that the scenery was rather boring. (Not that we recognized that word back then).

The tennis courts were still in use many years later. Today only the pay box hut and hard tennis courts remain and at the time of writing this they are in desperate need of renovation. After the Green Domino Restaurant closed in the 1940s, Leatherhead Depositories (a branch of Bishop & Sons Ltd) who had come to Leatherhead in the 1930s, relocated their offices from the High Street to Fetcham Grove, and remained there until the building was demolished in 1998. The site is now an office block called Cedar Court.

History tells us that Leatherhead Cricket Club was the first sporting club to play in this area, having been established around 1885. However the club can trace its history back to 1850. In 1865 the club became 'Leatherhead United C.C.' thereby combining the existing 'village' and 'amateur' teams. In the same year the club transferred from its original pitch on the Kingston Road recreational ground to a ground that would, some years later, become the London Transport Bus Garage.

Leatherhead Cricket Club Pavilion – Past.

Leatherhead Cricket Club Pavilion – Present.

About ten years later they moved across the road to the present ground beside the railway embankment. The 'United' was dropped in 1881. Leatherhead Cricket Club has a proud long history that includes many League and Cup successes. One of the author's fond memories is from the early 1950s when his father used to take him to see them play W.J. 'Bill' Edrich's 'Middlesex and England XI'. His side always included many prominent players of their day. 'Bill' Edrich was a very famous 'all-rounder' of his day. If you wish to know more about the clubs history a book was published to celebrate their 150th Anniversary 'Leatherhead Cricket Club 1850 - 2000'. We think the book is now out of print but a copy can be seen in Leatherhead Library.

Hockey was first played at Fetcham Grove in the early 1920s, when the Wesleyan Guild hired a pitch for their matches. It was not until 1985 that a group of Leatherhead Cricket Club members founded the Leatherhead Hockey Club. Soon after this the Leatherhead Ladies section was formed. Although the club no longer plays at Fetcham Grove, they are still in existence, which is a tribute to those who founded the club.

The 1910/1911 Leatherhead Directory states that the Leatherhead Lawn

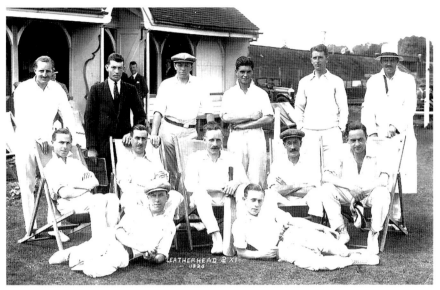

Leatherhead Cricket Club 2nd XI - 1928.
This is the only postcard we have of a Leatherhead CC Team.

Tennis Club was formed in 1908 and their courts were situated in a portion of the Leatherhead Cricket Ground. Just how long the original club existed we do not know. However, the courts remained there for many years. Today the Leatherhead Lawn Tennis Club founded in 1954 is based at Cannon Grove Fetcham.

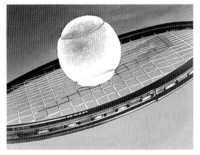

'Love all'

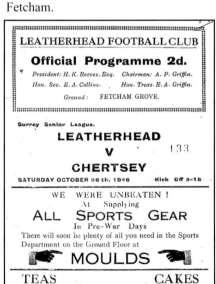

Leatherhead's first official programme season 1946-47.

One of your authors has followed the Leatherhead Football team, known as 'The Tanners', from a time 'when the skin was still on the animal'. He also has a collection of 'Tanners' memorabilia that almost covers the years described below.

Although football in Leatherhead can be traced back to the 1880s the current Leatherhead Football Club was formed in May 1946 with the merger of Leatherhead Rose and Leatherhead United. United had played at Fetcham Grove since 1927 when Herbert Reeves gave permission for them to use the pitch on his property. For this he was rewarded with the Club Presidency.

The new alliance started well, winning the Surrey Senior League four times in a row, followed by one season in the Metropolitan League, before becoming founder members of the Delphian League in 1951. They then progressed through the Corinthian and Athenian Leagues before finally joining the elite Isthmian League in 1972.

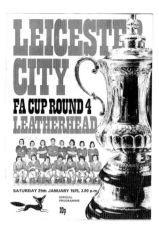

In 1969 they reached the semi-finals of the FA Amateur Cup, losing to eventual winners, Skelmersdale United and again in 1971, falling to Ilford.

In the 1974-75 season 'The Tanners' were national news with an FA Cup run that saw them beat Isthmian League rivals Bishops Stortford in round One Proper, then 3rd Division League side Colchester United in Round Two. It was Colchester United's first season back in theFootball League 3rd Division after a seven-year absence. In Round Three they beat 3rd Division Brighton 1-0 with a Chris Kelly individual special goal. In the Fourth Round they were drawn against 1st Division Leicester City at home. It remains the furthest the club has ever reached in the competition. With the game switched to Filbert Street, at the request of Tanners management, the BBC's Match of the Day covered the event and over 32,000 people were at the ground to see a dramatic match, in which the Tanners went two goals up through Peter McGillicuddy and Chris Kelly. The crowd then saw a Chris Kelly goal bound shot that would have made it 3-0 cleared off the line. Leicester City's fitness and class eventually told as the top team fought back to win 3-2 in the second half.

In 1978, the side reached the final of the FA Trophy, played at Wembley, only to lose 3-1 to Altrincham.

LEATHERHEAD F.C.

1977-78

Back Row *(left to right)* Dave Wall (coach), John Deary (physiotherapist), John Bailey, Colin Brooks, John Swannell, Dave Reid, Paul Whittaker, John Baker, Billy Salkeld, John Cooper, Billy Miller (manager).
Front Row *(left to right)* John Doyle, Micky Cook, Chris Kelly, Dennis Malley (captain), Ray Eaton, Barrie Davies, Kevin Mansell.

The 'Tanners' Football Team 1977-78. They went to Wembley and played Altrincham in the final of The FA Trophy unfortunately they lost 3-1. Their local hero, Chris Kelly (the lip) is 3rd from left, front row.

In 1996 Goff Powell wrote a book called 'Up the Tanners' recalling 50 years of following the ups and downs of Leatherhead FC. It is now out of print and a collector's item. However, if you wish to know more about the history of football in Leatherhead he suggests you read 'How Green is Mole Valley', by David Johnston and Graham Mitchell.

Following the end of the Second World War most towns and cities needed to get back to normality. The 1948 London Olympic Games, followed by the Festival of Britain in 1951, was probably the incentive for the formation of The Leatherhead and District Sports Association in February 1951.

It was comprised of individual members and local works clubs, with high hopes and much optimism. Its primary function: 'to establish, to foster, and to support schemes for the promotion of physical and social welfare of members by the organisation of amateur athletic sports meetings and such other sports activities as may from time to time be thought desirable'. The first Annual Athletic Meeting at Fetcham Grove took place the same year.

Although early programmes mention organisations and individuals, the programme for 1961 states 'that a men's club calling itself Leatherhead Athletic Club has become established this year', four years after the Leatherhead Ladies Athletic Club.

Leatherhead Men's AC c1960s.

Leatherhead Ladies' AC 1960s

One of the authors, himself a keen athlete, remembers a Leatherhead and District Scout Association Athletics Meeting being held there in 1953.

Did you know that in 1952 the L&DSA introduced baseball to Leatherhead? (Not a lot of people know that!) It was in conjunction with Sutton Beavers Baseball Club and held at the 'Grove' on the 26th July. It was billed as an international between ENGLAND versus CANADA. A report of the match in the Evening News, tells a somewhat different story. 'On 26 July 1952, a team representing England

Goff Powell receiving the Winner's Trophy from Phil Wright, District Chairman, at a local Scout Association Athletic Meeting c1953.

took on a squad from the Canadian military at the ground of Leatherhead Football Club. The English team comprised players from a trio of London-area clubs, the Mitcham Royals, Mitcham Tigers and Sutton Beavers'. The team was essentially an All-Star squad from the Western League, but it was given the 'England' moniker to help publicize the contest and it worked. The game which was played in Leatherhead attracted a sizable audience that included Walter Winterbottom, the England football coach. The All-Stars ultimately lost the contest 17-13.

The score was tied until the fifth innings, when Canada jumped ahead and held the lead despite 'two beautiful homers' by English players Frank Adey and Ray Reynolds, despite this the newspaper reported that "the Canadians told the British players they have a long way to go yet." However, it took another four years to come on a more regular basis. In 1956 a team called Leatherhead Maple Leafs played on the sports ground adjoining the main football ground. The team was comprised of former Epsom Lions players and other expatriate Canadians and Americans, plus a younger generation of local men interested in the game. Regrettably baseball only lasted a few years at the 'Grove', but it was a pleasure to watch.

Just to prove that it really did happen. But please read the text for clarification.

Leatherhead Maple Leafs c1950s.

Perhaps this next advert will rekindle happy memories for many readers when in 1953 the Leatherhead & District Sports Association held their first ever 'Good Friday Six-A-Side Football Tournament' at

the 'Grove', with Bookham 'A' being the eventual winners. It proved to be an instant success and became an annual event. At first it was only open to local clubs and organisations, but in the years that followed clubs from out of the area participated. It ran for nearly twenty years and was a 'family day out', people would arrive early and stay for the day, some even brought picnic lunches. One of the authors played for several clubs in this tournament, but never played in a final, only two semi-finals.

The programme cover says it all.

The Leatherhead Leisure Centre today.
It has undergone many changes since it opened in 1975.

Probably the coming of the Leisure Centre would be the most life changing experience for many of the local people, for it was to offer such a bewildering variety of facilities. The Centre, which had been under discussion since 1961, was eventually opened in 1975, and West Wing Swimming Pool was closed.

The Centre was extended in the 1980s with the erection of 'The Mole Barn' facility. In 1984, a Water Park was added, providing two lakes where instruction on sailing, boating, sail boarding, water skiing and canoeing could be given. Plans to build a new Centre on the site were drawn up by Mole Valley District Council prior to 2006, but instead the facility was given a 20-month, £12.6m refit and further extension, reopening (ten months late) in March 2011. The upgraded Centre includes a redesigned reception and entrance area. Today the lakes no longer exist and the Centre is run by Mole Valley District Council, in partnership with Fusion Lifestyle.

Leisure Centre Boating Lake.

There are at least three clubs still in existence from those early days. The Leatherhead Swimming Club, Junior Moles Badminton Club and The Mole Valley Indoor Bowling Club. A memory that remains in one of the authors mind is from the late 1970s and concerns the Leatherhead Basketball Team. They were originally the Crystal Palace Reserve Team and by coming to play at the Centre, duly adopted the 'town name' in their title. They did not stay for long, and moved on to another location away from the town.

Having now covered most of the main sports and leisure facilities offered by the area of Fetcham Grove, one must not forget the other major events held in the past such as the Leatherhead Carnival, Firework Displays, Car and Motorbike Rallies, Car Boots, Circuses and Bensons Fun Fair.

Oops! We nearly forgot, how many can recall Sunday 18th May 1980 when TVs 'Its A Knockout' came to town? The three competing teams were Bracknell v. Hertsmere v. Mole Valley. The Mole Valley team was Caroline Day, Richard Escott, David Mitchell, Fiona Pankhurst, Richard Piggott and Stuart Trussler. The eventual winners were Bracknell on 24 points, followed by Hertsmere on 22 and Mole Valley on 21 points. Because the programme was pre-recorded, it was not shown on TV until 13th June, thereby giving the contestants time to recover from any embarrassing moments that had occurred.

A typical 'It's A Knockout' competitive game.

We fully appreciate that after all this hectic activity you are ready to lie down in a darkened room, but please stay with us because we have to move on. At the end of the previous chapter we had a brief glimpse of our Town Bridge. We will now cross over it, looking at its interesting history and make our way up Bridge Street.

Chapter 3

THE TOWN BRIDGE AND MILL

Some of us will have crossed and re-crossed 'The Bridge' many times but have we ever given a thought to its history? The first thing to consider is that it is a work of art and is a structure that can 'stand its corner' with many a well-known contestant.

Yes, we know that the bridges crossing the Thames are loved and revered and very probably better known to the masses than our bridge, but that is what it is, 'our bridge'. It is a very fine brick structure with fourteen arches. If you have not already done so take a walk down Bridge Street to the small riverside terrace at the foot of Minchin Close. Just look at the bridge, admire the arches and count them. On a fine day it can be a peaceful spot. The traffic is not too intrusive, if you ignore the parked cars.

THE BRIDGE — LEATHERHEAD

With a little imagination this early 'photo' (late 19th century) might be a water colour by John Constable. The mill is to the right. Note the rather 'rickety' looking footbridge. In the background a telegraph pole is visible, on the railway embankment.

How long has there been a crossing on this site? It is thought that the river has been crossed at the present site for very many years and in all probability it was active before the Norman Conquest. That is the date engraved in our psyche, even your authors know that the encounter took place in 1066 at a Sussex town called Battle, now that's an original name.

Like most river crossings in fairly shallow waters, the first one would have been a ford. Indeed the name of our town does not, as local myth would have it, have anything to do with the leatherworking tradition, but it originated very much further back in time. In AD 880 King Alfred bequeathed an estate in the area known as 'Leodridan'. The name 'Lered' has also been used. Language specialists have provided a number of alternative meanings and one of them is 'a ford'.

We read about fords but seldom do we give a thought to the trouble and strife that would manifest itself in the winter months when all access would be impossible. Remember the floods of 1968 when even advanced beings such as us were well and truly 'snookered'.

Wherever a camera is produced a crowd appears, well not quite.
This picture, dated 1907, gives a splendid view of the track leading to the mill.

We are told that in the 1280s the bridge was maintained by 'the neighbourhood'. By 1361 alms were being collected for repairs. In 1418 we know that the 'Bridge Wardens held an acre in the common field', an asset that provided some income for upkeep of the bridge. By the 15th century and early 16th century this land, which comprised three and a half acres, had made regular contributions to the maintenance costs.

By the 16th century the bridge had acquired gates at both ends. The good folk of Fetcham and Leatherhead who had contributed to its upkeep would have been issued with their own keys. Was there a lucrative 'key borrowing business' we wonder?

Throughout the early years of its existence, many people would have continued to use the ford that was on the up-stream side of the bridge. Not only could this have been more convenient, in the summer months of course, but the wooden wheels used on horse drawn vehicles had a tendency to dry out and their spokes and felloes would work loose. The ford not only caused the wood to swell and tighten, but the horse could also take a well-deserved drink. All those photographs of horses and carts in a ford or stream, surely evoke those well-known lines 'what is this life, if full of care, we have no time to stand and stare'.

By 1774 the Surrey Justices considered that parts of the bridge were in such a state that they could cause injury to the public. It was recommended that the bridge should be repaired and enlarged. The meetings and discussions concerning the repairs and rebuild were rather protracted, does this sound familiar, and it was not until 1782 that an Act of Parliament made the County responsible for the Leatherhead Bridge and others in the County.

No time was lost in carrying out the work and George Gwilt the County Surveyor had overall responsibility. The task was completed in 1782/1783. The bridge was widened and the parapets, which were capped with Portland stone, were provided with pedestrian refuges. The bricks above the arches contained second-hand bricks that were reputed to have come from Ashtead Park.

If you care to look under the arches (no need to go for a paddle) you will see the joins in the brick work where the bridge was widened on the Southern Side. Another of Mr. Gwilt's bridges spanned the Mole at Downside, Cobham. Unfortunately this bridge was not as lucky as ours, because it was swept away in the vicious floods of 1968. Evidence of a medieval bridge can be found under nine of the arches at Leatherhead.

Although this photo was taken in the 1930s the view from the same spot today is almost unaltered. You can see the chimney from the original Pumping Station in Waterway Road. Note some of the town's youth sitting on the parapet. (Teenagers had yet to be 'invented').

Provided that you have now crossed over the bridge with us you will find yourself at the bottom of Bridge Street. We will walk along the river bank for a short distance, (on the Southern side) at the bottom of Minchin Close, where we will very soon be standing on the site of the Town Mill.

The Domesday Book tells us that there were twenty watermills along the banks of the River Mole. Today there are very few remains of these essential establishments visible on the ground. The oldest mill on the river is said to be Sidlow Mill on the outskirts of Reigate. The mill at Leatherhead also goes far back in time, possibly to the time of the Roman Conquest. It was powered by a fairly large 'undershot' wheel. That is one where the power is produced by the water passing under the wheel. A strong, reliable current is needed and this was ensured by the design of the 'mill race'. The flow could be turned off by lowering a set of sluice gates.

During its long life the mill served a number of different purposes. It not only performed the rather obvious task of grinding flour. For many years Leatherhead was well known as a prominent Leather Tanning Centre. Soaking baths and bark crushing rollers operated alongside the flour mill and two of the bark crushing rollers can be seen in The Leatherhead Museum. They were discovered when the mill site was being tidied up as Minchin Close was being developed.

From this point in time it is difficult to imagine the sounds and smells that would have been evident. Those of you that went to Kingston during the time that leather tanning was being carried out there, will in all probability, still be able to recall the foul smell that enveloped the town at certain times. Perhaps our mill being 'in the country' would not have been so bad, but there again the good folk back then would no doubt have been used to the pungent aroma, which would have mingled with

25

This 'photo' from 1905 is an idyllic scene, with the horse and cart standing in the river. The barn, in the background, housed the swimming pool used by St. John's School. The undershot mill wheel looks as if it has seen better days.

other, not so fragrant smells. The creaking of the timbers, the smell of freshly ground flour and the jingle of horse harnesses would have completed the scene.

In more recent times (c1890) one of the buildings was converted into a swimming pool. In 1900 St. John's School took over the facilities. So there you have it, this end of the town has been associated with 'aqueous exercise' for many years. The mill, it could be said, was the fore-runner of the Leisure Centre, but with a less sophisticated water treatment system.

During the Second World War the 'Dig for Victory' campaign was enthusiastically embraced and every piece of spare land was put under the spade. The islands on the South Side of the bridge did not escape and allotments were established on them. At the time these islands were linked by a footbridge. All the usual vegetables were grown there, but bearing in mind that these islands flooded

The Old Mill 1938

This NS type bus, on the 418 route has had a 'little mishap'.
Lady Passenger:- "I say my good man is this bus going to Epsom?"
Conductor: - "Well Madam that was our intention."

on occasion perhaps rice would have been a more appropriate crop.

We have now completed this part of our journey, but before we move on up Bridge Street, let us indulge ourselves in a little bit of fantasy.

Before Railways had been developed as a serious means of mass transport and motorways were not even a figment of one's imagination, water was an important means of transporting goods in bulk at an acceptable price. The canal system had been well developed by the early 19th century. In fact the River Wey had been made navigable by 1658 with further improvements being carried out in 1671. Leatherhead was not to be left out of this drive for increased prosperity and plans to make the River Mole navigable were first mooted in 1664 and later in 1698.

The plans envisaged vessels of 'twenty tons burthen' which would carry timber, coal, corn and any other bulk commodity that could prove economical. However it was not until 1827 that a grand plan was proposed to build a canal joining Portsmouth with London. Below is an extract from 'Priestley's Historical Account of Navigable, Rivers & Canals 1831'.

In the year 1827, a plan was devised by Nicholas Wilcox Cundy, Engineer for the construction of a canal from London to Portsmouth, to be called "The Grand Imperial Ship Canal" by which it was stated, the largest ships would have been enabled

Someone with a sense of humour published this post card to reflect what might have been.

to perform a passage, from one of these ports to the other, by the aid of steam towage, in about sixteen hours. The canal was to have been extended from the Thames at Rotherhithe, in a South-West direction across the Centre of the County of Surrey, by Leatherhead and Dorking to Alford, on the border of Sussex; and thence by Pulborough and Chichester to Portsmouth; a distance, altogether, of seventy four miles. Its width was to be one hundred and fifty feet; and its depth of water was always to be twenty eight feet: There were to be four locks, each three hundred feet long and sixty-four feet broad. It was alleged by Mr. Cundy, that the canal would be completed within four years, at an expense not exceeding four million pounds; and that it would produce revenue of seven million pounds a year. However, the attempt to form a Company that could carry this design to fruition was not successful.

In hindsight we can be glad that the scheme came to nought. Just imagine all those forty-ton Lorries thundering along the M25 making their way to Leatherhead Docks, dream on!

It's time for us to continue on our journey; luckily we don't have to thunder round the M25 to do so. We will make our way up Bridge Street along the North Side, or left hand side and look at the changes that have taken place over the years. We might be amazed by the variety of diverse businesses that existed.

Chapter 4

THE FOOT OF THE BRIDGE, ON THE TOWN SIDE

Apart from the town itself, the bottom of Bridge Street would have been a busy place, back in those days of yore. Not only was the mill a place of comings and goings, but the ford and the bridge would be the point of access for all those horse drawn vehicles and pedestrians with a desire to enter or leave our fair town from the West. From our modern perspective it would have been fascinating to just sit and watch the activity, taking in the sights and sounds, not forgetting the smells that would have filled a balmy summer's day.

The River Mole was also used as a ford. The picture shows the delivery cart of John Symonds, Butcher of the High Street, no doubt allowing drink for the horse and cooling the wheels of the cart before moving on to Fetcham.

If you are the member of a long standing Leatherhead family you might just have caught a glimpse of one of your ancestors putting the world to rights, but enough of this romantic dreaming we must get on.

Before we make our way up Bridge Street we will take one of those short detours along the Northern river bank. Today Emlyn Lane is a cul-de-sac, but thirty years or so ago the lane would have formed a junction with the bottom of Bridge Street, where the mini roundabout is now. From the accompanying photographs we can see that this area was a hive of industry. Incidentally the 1910/1911 Directory calls it River Lane; perhaps it was changed to Emlyn Lane to avoid confusion with River Lane off Randalls Road. A more likely reason is that in medieval times the River Mole was known as the Emlyn Stream.

Incidentally Mrs. Joy Playford worked in one of the engineering workshops there, during the Second World War, and when talking to one of the authors, she referred to it by this first name. In the 1940 Street Directory it is called River Lane but ten years later it's called Emlyn Lane.

At the junction there once stood the offices of The Leatherhead Building Company. They were a well-known business in the local area and beyond. In 1937 they built a new shop and library facility in the High Street for Boots the Chemist. They also secured the contract to convert some other premises in the High Street into modern shops. Modern by 1930s standards that is.

Next door to the Leatherhead Building Company were the premises of K.R. Wigley & Company Limited. They specialised in a wide variety of engineering activities. These included welded fabrications and machined components. One of their lesser known activities was specialist vehicle conversions for some of the well-known motor manufacturers including Ford and Austin. The business was started by Ken Wigley just before the Second World War. In 1953 Harold Bushell joined Ken and in 1957 the company was formed as a Development and Manufacturing Engineering business. They also carried out sub-contract work for local companies, including Neil & Spencer, Ronson and Goblin. They also had premises in Church Road.

The town Fire Station once stood on the bend in the lane. It was opened in 1926 and superseded the 'Clock Tower' facilities in North Street. The first fire appliance to occupy the new station was manufactured by the Merryweather Company. It was named 'Margaret Blades', she was the daughter of Sir Rowland Blades who performed the opening ceremony. He later became The Lord Mayor of London.

The 'new' Fire Station in Emlyn Lane on the opening day in 1926.

In 1932 a second appliance was acquired. It was manufactured by Dennis Motors of Guildford. They were the Country's largest manufacturer of fire engines at that time and today their specialist vehicles are still serving many local authorities. The company has now become part of a worldwide organisation and their buses can be seen in Hong Kong and Kingston to name just two locations. This second engine was named 'Margaret Rose' by Mrs Greville of Polesden Lacey fame. She was the Godmother of Princess Margaret, the sister of our Queen.

Leatherhead Fire Brigade – This photograph is reported to have been taken around the time of the building of the new Fire Station. Judging by the number of firemen Leatherhead was well served.

The Fire Station and its fire fighters served the local community faithfully for over forty years but by the 1960s it was obvious that the premises were no longer suited to the modern needs. In 1969 a new Fire Station was opened in Cobham Road, so that when the 'bell rang' it was no longer necessary for the larger vehicles to negotiate the tight bend and parked cars in Belmont Road. (The Fire Engines did not exit the old premises via the Bridge Street Junction).

Persons of a certain age might remember that the station was not always fully manned and when 'a shout' was on, it was necessary to call up the manpower. This was done by sounding the 'air raid siren' that was located on the roof of the Burton building, now the Travelodge Hotel, above Argos. The sound carried far and wide and with a northerly wind the good folk of Mickleham would have been 'well informed'. A southerly wind would have carried the Dorking sound their way.

Next to the Fire Station was a small building with a large ventilator on the roof. The 1910/1911 Town Directory shows it to be the Town Mortuary. It

The Leatherhead Fire Station under water during the 1968 flood. The old Jehovah's Witnesses Kingdom Hall can just be seen on the left hand side.

was The Coroners Mortuary, and was used to process all those persons who had died in a location other than a hospital. It was not used after the 1968 floods had occurred. The building was demolished in 1987 when Holly Court was built. Earlier records show that the mortuary had been located in the kennels of 'Whyteleafe' in Bridge Street. We will be visiting these premises a little later on in this chapter.

On the corner of Emlyn Lane we can see the Jehovah's Witnesses Church Hall. They previously had a hut on the same site. The

Emlyn Lane 1965

present modern building dates from the mid-1990s. At one time a building close to Kingdom Hall was occupied by The Leatherhead Press, who had previously been at Lower Fairfield Road and prior to that Oak Road off the Kingston Road.

Emlyn Lane, the 1968 floods showing Wigley's Yard.

The new offices between the Church and Bridge Street stand on the site of cottages and a wooden structure that was home to another engineering workshop, called Crescent Gauges. They specialised in sub-contracting parts for many companies both local and further afield, including Hawkers at Kingston and Vickers-Armstrongs at Brooklands, Weybridge.

Chapter 5

OUR JOURNEY UP BRIDGE STREET ALONG THE NORTHERN SIDE

Before we begin our journey it might be an appropriate time for us to pause and reflect on Leatherhead's past, Although we do not propose to go back into the dark ages we will, at some locations, be considering what our town was like in the 18th century and occasionally beyond.

The development of the town is well documented by many sources, but here are a few interesting snippets from the letters and observations made by the Revd. James Dallaway who was the Vicar of Leatherhead from 1804 until 1834. He says, 'The village, much to my regret, is rapidly losing its primary character and converting itself into a multiplication of considerable houses, into an appendage of the enormous London, although nature has placed them at twenty miles distance from each other'. He also talks about our Town Bridge, 'At the termination of that in the direct road to Guildford, is the handsomest bridge over any part of the river, which consists of fourteen arches'. (You will remember that we had a good look at the bridge in Chapter Three.)

The Rev. James Dallaway, distinguished antiquarian and Vicar of Leatherhead
1804 - 1834.

We also learn that in the 19th century the following trades and businesses could be found in Leatherhead; Coach Builders, Booksellers, Blacksmiths, Butchers, Grocers, Tanners, Bakers, Bookmakers, Fishmongers, Saddlers, Surgeons, Carpenters, together with Clockmakers, Milliners, Maltsters, Tailors and others, including a Chemist and Stay maker. (Just try to imagine the sounds and smells that those activities would generate.)

The town was also located at the centre of two important transport links. The main road from London to Horsham and the South Coast crossed the East West route from Kent to Guildford and beyond and as a result the 19th century village was very prosperous.

To list all the changes to the shops and businesses over the years would be an impossible task, so we decided to include digestible information that will give the reader an indication as to how the street contributed to the town's history.

We continue our journey up Bridge Street, to the town crossroads. Where the car park is now, just before the Running Horse public house, there stood a row of four cottages. These were Nos. 46, 44, 42 and 40 and the photograph shows the rear view. To date no photo of the front view has emerged but the picture, dating from 1905, shows Henry Skilton's builders yard.

The left hand 'photo', circa late1950s, shows the garden wall in front of the cottages next to the Running Horse. In the right hand 'photo', taken from the railway bridge, we can see Skilton's Yard and the back of the cottages that were located behind the wall shown in the left hand picture.

We now arrive at The Running Horse public house, just to look at you understand, but if all the walking has made you thirsty please feel free and leave one behind the bar for Goff and Brian! Much has already been written about the famous building and we feel that we can do no better than to repeat Goff Powell's description contained in his book entitled 'The Inns and Public Houses of Leatherhead and District' (please see the Bibliography list.)

The Running Horse, which was probably a private cottage, dates from the 15th century and there is a reference to it in a lease of 1414. It is best known as the alehouse immortalized by the poet John Skelton in his poem 'The Tunning of Elinour Rumming' who was supposed to be the alewife at the Inn in the 16th century. In 1525 she was fined 2d for selling ale at excessive prices. Another story is that she would put chicken and rat droppings into the ale 'to give it body'. The locals found out about this and put her in a barrel and rolled her into the river.

Ye Olde Running Horse c1909.
As with all the early 'photos', it is the lack of traffic that takes our attention.

(Why waste time with legal proceedings?) Although there is no firm evidence of her living at the Inn or even that it was an ale house at the time, it makes a nice piece of folklore.

The Running Horse in more recent times.

Any old pub worth its salt will have a royal connection and 'The Runner' is no exception.

There is a legend that the pub was named by Queen Elizabeth 1. She was on one of her 'progresses' and was halted by floods, the dear old Mole was throwing another 'wobbly'. She was desirous to get a message to her next port of call. A rider was summoned and executed his task with commendable speed and Her Majesty said, "From henceforth this hostelry shall be called The Running Horse." We don't claim this is necessarily an historic fact, but you find a better story.

In the early days the Inn had many owners. The Directories of the late 1880s refer to the Inn being called 'the Old Running Horse'. For many years it was called 'Ye Old Running Horse'. In 1889, George Moore of the 'Swan' bought the 'Runner' in an auction. The longest running tenants were the Castleman family, who ran the Inn for over sixty years. During the mid-19th century, another Inn called the 'New

Elinour Rumming – warts and all.

This picture is taken from a postcard dated 1938, it shows the sign before the damage.

Running Horse' was built across the road, but within ten years it was just a 'beer and lodging house'.

During the Second World War a Canadian soldier fired a bullet at the pub sign and the damage was evident for many years until a new sign was erected. Before the D-Day landings the town and the surrounding area was home to very many Canadian soldiers. Cometh the hour they, together with other allies and all their equipment vanished, just like the early morning mist, before the summer sunrise.

The Canadians, however did leave us a more fitting legacy, the road we now call Young Street was built by

This photograph shows Mr. King the Prime Minister of Canada officially opening the road on the 28th August 1941.

Canadian solders based here to enable military vehicles to avoid bottlenecks of places like Redhill, Reigate and Leatherhead. The road was finished in the summer of 1941. It was years later the name Young Street was adopted; it was named after Major Young who was in charge of the soldiers who built it.

Although the pub has changed landlords many times since the Castleman era, it was pleasing to see a local family, the Huddlestones take up occupancy. Alas Roy died in June 2012. Colin and Daniela Turner are the Landlords at the time of writing.

Next to the Running Horse in the early 1920s and up to the mid 1930s No. 36 was occupied by William Budden, Fishmonger, however, he had opposition across the street at No. 35. Maybe there was not enough trade for two Fishmongers, because by 1936 he is listed as a General Dealer and later as a Scrap Metal Merchant. By the 1950s Harry Reed occupies the premises and later trades as D & K Reed Ltd (Reed Brothers) Motor Spares and Repair Service. It is possible that some readers may still remember the brothers trading under the name East Surrey Caravans in Belmont Road. The older building has been demolished and replaced by Connaught House and is home to the Surrey Football Association.

We now come to one of the 'architectural jewels' in the street. This terrace is one of those 'taken for granted' structures. Most of us that are local will have no doubt passed by it on numerous occasions and never given it a second glance.

Alas that is often the fate of those buildings that fit naturally into their surroundings.

This terrace, Nos. 34 to 28, was built in 1810 on the site of the Poor House. The builder was a well-known Leatherhead resident named Benjamin Simmons, who lived from 1751 to 1832. He came to Leatherhead around 1765. Benjamin was apprenticed to Abraham Elliott, who operated his carpentry and building business from premises at the top end of Church Walk. Sometime after 1782 Benjamin was able to acquire the business.

The business flourished and the company built a number of houses in the area. Benjamin was a great supporter of the Leatherhead Parish Church. He was the Tower Captain for many years and if you are able to visit the 'Ringing Chamber' you will see that his name appears on a number of the 'Peal Boards'. In 1792 the ring of bells in the church tower was increased from six to eight and Benjamin was the driving force behind this project. In 1877 the ring was increased to the current ten bells.

This fine terrace would be 'at home' in any one of our Cathedral Cities. Next time you are passing spend a moment to take in the fine architectural features.

It records that in 1795 a peal 'Oxford Treble Bob' containing 6400 changes was rung in 3 hours 50 minutes. Benjamin rung No. 2 bell and conducted the peal.

As an added interest, it is highly probable that Admiral Lord Nelson of Trafalgar fame, visited the premises at the top of Church Walk. Documentation exists to corroborate this possibility.

The Leatherhead Museum has extensive information about Benjamin Simmons and the buildings constructed by his company, thanks to the research that was carried out by Alun Roberts a fellow member of the L&DLHS.

For many years the terrace was residential and in the 19th century 'well to do' families would have been comfortably off and had some domestic help, ranging from a 'ladies maid' and possibly a 'butler'.

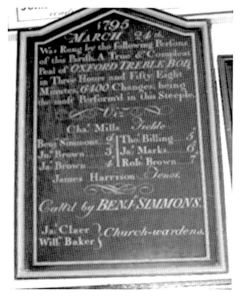

This is a Peal Board that hangs in the Ringing Chamber in The Parish Church.

In 1950 Mrs. C N Wolf opened a small Secretarial School in Ashtead. She moved to No. 28 in 1950 and established the Leatherhead Secretarial School. The business was successful and in 1978 she acquired Nos. 30 and 32.

The Leatherhead School of Music was established in 1926 at Devon House, on the corner of Church Road and Poplar Road, by two sisters Elsie and Mabel Fuller. They taught piano, strings, and elocution to a very high standard. Later Devon House was sold and Mrs. Wolf offered the School accommodation in No. 28 'The Terrace' by which time Sheila Hind was the principal. Elsie Fuller died in 1944 but Mabel ran the School until 1962 when she decided to retire. Many an aspiring musician was enthused by the devotion of Miss Mabel Fuller and her devoted staff.

The School of Music closed in the early 1990s and the Secretarial School followed soon afterwards.

Today the terrace is mainly used for office accommodation and Nos. 28, 30 and 32 are now called

Stonebridge House. With its garden wall, steps and railings it is a Grade II listed building recognizing its special architectural and historic interest. In the 1970s UCS (Universal Car Spares) occupied No. 34 mainly for tyre sales.

Our next port of call is No. 26. Today No. 26 Bridge Street is known as Century House and for many years has been used for business purposes. Originally it was called Rose Cottage and in the early 1900s was home to Dr. Walter Carrington Hearnden, Physician & Surgeon. Around 1906 Dr. Sidney James Ormond joined him in the practice. Soon after this   Dr. Hearnden moved to Elm House, North Street. Dr. Ormond remained there until about 1931, before moving to Linden House, Epsom Road.

Following his departure the house underwent major changes and became a cafe.

Being close to the River Mole Bridge, it was aptly named the Bridge Cafe, it even had its own cake shop at the front of the building. The photograph below on the right shows Lloyd Loom furniture in the cafe. The Lloyd Loom process was invented in 1917 by the American Marshall B. Lloyd, who twisted Kraft paper round a metal wire, placed the paper threads on a loom and wove them into what was to become the traditional Lloyd Loom fabric. Lloyd Loom original furniture is highly sort after. What price today, for those in the picture?

However, it was short lived and by the late 1940s it had become The New Bridge Cafeteria (the Bridge was

BRIDGE CAFE (L'head) Ltd.

26 BRIDGE STREET

SPECIAL TOURIST LUNCHEON   **2/3**
Morning Coffee — Dainty Teas — An interesting departure in Cafe Restaurants Ask for our Mauve or Orange rooms, where you will enjoy a Luncheon or Tea during your tour daintily served

Telephone Leatherhead 489

Business card showing the cottage as it would have looked in the early 20th century.

The Bridge Café, Leatherhead.

The Bridge Café, Leatherhead—The Mauve Room.

These 1940s advertising cards show external and internal views of the Bridge Cafeteria.

not new!). It eventually assumed the name Sky High Catering House, the owner being S. J. Palmer who also owned the Sky High Cafe at No. 13 Bridge Street.

On the left hand side of Bridge Street next to Rose Cottage (No. 26) once stood the premises of Venthams Garage (Nos. 24 and 22). Charles Ventham a Coach Painter by trade was born in Winchester, estimated date 1816 and following his apprenticeship with the celebrated Coachbuilder Jones of Southampton he went to live in London, where he set up in business. He married Jane Simmonds

An early photograph showing Ventham's works. What price the vintage car today?

who was an Umbrella Maker and they bore a son Edward, born 1842 at North Audley Street, Middlesex. They must have moved to Leatherhead soon after Edward was born because according to the 1851 census they had two further children Jane in 1844 and Charles in 1846 both born in Leatherhead.

Charles established his coach building business on this site in 1849 making high quality carriages. His wife Jane died in 1859 and Charles in 1879, neither lived to see the business flourish. Following their father's death the sons, Edward and Charles continued the business.

Despite the decline in coach travel due to the expansion of the railways, the company continued to make commissioned vehicles. Press cuttings of the period confirm that the company had a world-

wide reputation. In 1882 they purchased the Dorking Coach Building concern of the late Israel Walker.

Young Charles died in 1889 and following the death of Edward in 1901, his widow Melissa Ann ran the business, she was later joined by their son Edward and he was the main instigator in bringing the company into the 20th century and the age of the motor car. A garage was established and they also produced bodywork for Daimler and Armstrong Siddeley cars. Around 1909 the company applied to become official RAC repairers.

In 1929 the company exhibited two of their coaches in their showroom, which attracted the attention of circus owner Bertram Mills. Although it is said he purchased one of them, no actual record of this can be found. The business finally closed in 1936 due to Edward's continuing ill-health, he and his wife Rose Marian retired to Bognor Regis. He died two years later, but his widow retained and leased the property until her death in 1980, when it passed to her niece, who sold it several years later to a property developer. Prior to this the site was for many years occupied by Motor and Air

Ventham's yard circa early 1930s.
The Petrol Pump in the centre of the picture behind the lamp post can now be seen in the garden of the Leatherhead Museum as the picture on the right shows. It is painted bright red – sorry no colour.

Products Ltd, Plastics Fabricators and later LMC Panels. The site was cleared in 1985 and the Coach House Court office complex built.

The only surviving building from the Venthams era is the early 19th century cottage that can be seen in the 1930s photograph. You can just see the Garage on the right hand side. In front of the house just behind the lamp post there is a hand operated petrol pump. It is now in the garden of

No. 24 and 22 Bridge Street c1980s.

Leatherhead Museum at Hampton Cottage, Church Street. One of the authors friends lived in the house in the 1950s and he can remember playing at being a 'petrol pump attendant'. He is still a big kid at heart, because he enjoys telling visitors this story when he is on steward's duty at the Museum.

They say 'if you can remember the swinging 60s you were not there'. We think that this is because many of us that were there found ourselves far too busy bringing up families and attending to other mundane tasks.

However, Leatherhead did feature in 'the swinging sixties', so ladies, find those flared skirts and starched petticoats and gentlemen where is the 'Teddy Boy' gear?

Now, why have we made this request, because we are going clubbing, although back in those days it was not referred to as such. No. 22a was home to the 'Chuck Wagon' Club. It started life in a Nissan hut at the rear of the premises reached via Chitty's Alley. Sometime later it became known as the 'Bluesette Club', following a mysterious fire. How often are these fires mysterious? The owners instigated a rebuild.

In 1965 drummer Chris Townson and singer Andy Ellison formed a local band called the Clockwork

CHUCK WAGON
22A, BRIDGE STREET
LEATHERHEAD

FEBRUARY 26th
FOLK CONCERT

BOYD RIVERS and
GERRY LAUGHRAN
Blues Harmonica and Guitar
Jazz and Folk Club membership
2/6
Lunch and Snacks served daily

BLUESETTE CLUB
THE SILENCE
SUN. 13ᵗʰ MAR. 5/- 7.30-11

Onions, which later became The Few, and then The Silence. This band consisted of Townson and Ellison, with Geoff McClelland on guitar and John Hewlett on bass guitar.

In 1966, Chris Townson met The Yardbird's Manager, Simon Napier-Bell, and invited him to come and see The Silence at The Burford Bridge Hotel. Napier-Bell described them as "positively the worst group I'd ever seen," but still agreed to manage them. He changed their name to John's Children, dressed them up in white stage outfits and encouraged them to be outrageous to attract the attention of the press. He named the band after bass player John Hewlett, Napier-Bell co-wrote 'Smashed Blocked' with John Hewlett, but because of his lack of confidence in the band's musical abilities, he used session musicians on the recording. To his surprise 'Smashed Block/Strange Affair' broke into the US Billboard hot 100 and reached local top ten charts in Florida and California. In late 1966 the band bought the Bluesette Club with the proceeds from this US Hit, and they renamed the venue The John's Children Club.

John's Children including Marc Bolan on the right.

In March 1967 Napier-Bell replaced guitarist Geoff McClelland with Marc Bolan. Yes! The same Marc Bolan who went on to form glam rock band T. Rex. In the same year they made their UK Debut with their own composition 'Just What You Want'. During his time with the band, Bolan is said to have lodged near our Parish Church of St. Mary & St. Nicholas. Buying the club also gave the group the opportunity to choose the artists that would perform there. The likes of Jimi Hendrix, Cat Stevens, Graham Bond and Simon Dupree to name but some. The club soon gained a reputation as the haunt of just about every villain in the town. John's Children were active for less than two years and were not very successful commercially, having released six singles and only one album. But they had a big influence on punk rock and are seen by some as the precursors of glam rock. In retrospect the band has been praised for the impact they had and their singles have become amongst the most sought after British 1960 rock collectables. And you thought that you lived in a sleepy country town!

In 1967 Peter Keary established his upholstery business and soon after this he acquired the building. In later years the business moved to Old Station Approach, off Randalls Road. He was an accomplished non-league footballer playing for several local clubs including Leatherhead.

At No. 22 during the early part of the 20th century and for many years, the premises was a hairdresser's once occupied by William Starley, followed by William Surh, Jesse Davies and finally M. Freeman.

In the 1960s Martin Brown & Co Estate Agents shared the premises with R. Kenber, Solicitor. Between then and now various businesses have occupied the premises including Carousel Boutique, Pretty Pieces Giftware shop, then Kevin White Photographic Studio, Greens Picture Frames and Mirrors. Black Dog Gallery & Picture Framers the current owners arrived in 2003.

At the turn of the 20th century No. 20 was Robert Smith's Bakery, within five years he was followed by John Harvey Sheath. However, by 1930 the smell of fresh bread disappeared and was replaced by that of fresh fruit, Ernest Marshall Clarke purchased the property and it became a Fruiterers. The shop remained in the family for many years. One of the authors recalls going into the shop with a list of items for his Mum, but unfortunately she had not given him enough to pay for them. Mr. Clarke duly said "don't worry son your Mum can pay me the difference next time she comes in."

Times were different then. To-day the former shop forms part of the 'flat' complex known as Bridge Place.

At No. 18 we find an interesting variety of occupations. Over a hundred years ago George Beams the Boot Maker would have catered for your footwear needs. In the 1918 Street Directory Mrs. Ellen Burchell the Blouse Maker is in occupancy of No. 18. By the 1920s the shop becomes a Tobacconist and Confectioners run by Mrs. Lillian Birch and remained in this type of business for many years, various owners have been Mrs. Mogridge, Lawrence Dutt, Percy Turton, A. Girdler and Allwood's.

Another enterprising business to occupy the shop was Jay Music Services who sold string and wind instruments together with sheet music. The shop also forms part of the 'flat' complex known as Bridge Place.

c 1930s

The sustenance of the inner man and woman was not forgotten. In 1911, No. 16 was home to Joseph Lack's Grocery Store, he was followed in the early 1930s by (1934)

Lack's Stores c1911

Bridge Street c1911.

Stevenson & Rush Ltd., Grocers and Provision Merchants who remained until the early 1970s, when the type of business was carried on by Oakshotts Ltd. Both the authors seem to remember a shop selling clocks from this site. It had a lovely stylised clock on the outside of the building, however, the name of the shop eludes them. In the early 1980s Homeflair, English Craftsmen-Made Furniture was sold here. Later W.E.H. Nunn, Men's Outfitters, relocated from the High Street. Today the premises offer you tanning and beauty treatment by Sunshine Indoors. What will they think of next? .

Robt. A. Whittle, High-Class Draper for Everything.

Smart Up-to-Date Millinery at London Prices.

Dressmaking our Special Department.

Why not give us a Trial?

Agent for Dr. Jaeger's Wool Undergarments for Ladies and Children.

Also Achille Serre High-Class Dyeing and Cleaning.

We stock Viyella.

Bridge Street, LEATHERHEAD.

Wm. BEAKE,
Draper, Millinery, and Dressmaking.

BRIDGE ST., LEATHERHEAD.

Household Linens, Underclothing.
HORROCKSES LONGCLOTHS, *All Stamped with Name.*

Sole Agent in this District for
JAEGER'S UNDERCLOTHING
FOR LADIES' AND CHILDREN'S WEAR.
Full priced Catalogues sent on application.

DRESS MATERIALS in Great Variety. *Patterns sent on application.*
Hosiery, Gloves, Belts.

"AZA" Stocked in various Patterns for Blouses.
Pyjamas, Shirts, etc., and Children's Underclothing.

No. 14 and No. 12 Bridge Street has had a chequered history. In the early part of the 20th century it was a Drapers shop run by Robert Whittle and then William Beake.

Later in the 1920s the shop was divided into two when Flinn & Son Ltd., Dyers & Cleaners, took up occupancy of No. 14 and remained there until the 1940s. Alexander Chugg an Optician moved into No. 12 but by the mid-1930s and into the 1940s John May, Electrical Engineer is listed as being there. The 1950s then see the beginning of the premises being used as an eating house. In the 1950 Kelly's Directory it is just listed as A. Turner, Café, but both the authors remember it as

For a good meal before or after the match, eat at
Leatherhead's Newest Restaurant

THE REGENT

12/14, BRIDGE STREET, LEATHERHEAD
ENGLISH & CONTINENTAL CUISINE———————
FULLY LICENSED UNTIL 11.30 p.m.
RESERVATIONS — LEATHERHEAD 3436
(We can cater for parties up to 50 in number)

The Primrose Café. They served up a very tasty 'brunch', just the meal to impress a young lady in those innocent days of yore, well it worked for us. Later The Primrose expanded into No. 14 when it became vacant. By the early 1970s it became The Regent offering English and Continental Cuisine.

The ownership has changed many times since then, such as the Shahee Mahal Tandoori Restaurant, the Standard Tandoori, Mole Wine Bar & Bistro, the Piccolo Paradiso Italian Restaurant, the Mombay Spice, and at the time of writing this it is the Five Rivers Indian Restaurant.

The occupants of No. 12a in the 1966 Street Directory were Ann's Ladies Hairdresser, Mayers & White Ltd. Dental Laboratories. On the Second Floor was Mr. F.L. Mills (B.D.S) Dental Surgery along with Dental Technicians. The Technicians also had rooms on the third floor. Six years later only Mayers & White and Mr. Mills remained. Both occupied the premises for many years after.

Kingsnorth's Bakers and Confectioners decorated for the Coronation of Edward VII 1902.

We know that there was a Baker plying his trade from the premises of No. 10 Bridge Street in the 1880s and most probably before then. During the 1880s Frederick Kingsnorth was the Baker and he remained there until the early 1920s when the business was taken over by Cecil Whitehead. In the early 1930s Wren's (Klaren Ltd) bought the business. They were followed by J & R Morgan, the Holmes family and finally Harrington's. One a penny, two a penny, Hot Cross Buns. Remember the days when you could only get them on Good Friday.

Those of you who have lived in Leatherhead for some time will recall the sudden and sad demise of Harrington's Bakery. However, who can forget that wonderful smell of freshly baked bread and their beautiful cakes, the early morning queues and the friendly counter staff. Maybe some of you

HARRINGTONS
BAKERS : CONFECTIONERS

Master Bakers in Leatherhead
for 35 years
8 & 10, Bridge Street, Leatherhead.
Tel : 01372 372195

This lovely artist's impression of the shop is from a leaflet 'Visit Leatherhead' (Town Centre Promotions Ltd). A fitting reminder of how the premises once looked.

remember Elsie Kirkham, who joined the staff as a young lady and worked in the shop for many years?

By now we will have seen that providing clothing of the male body featured amongst the Leatherhead businesses and we find that No. 8 Bridge Street will not disappoint us. From around 1905 to 1911 William Dickenson a Tailor was in residence.

He was succeeded by Edgar Foster who in the 1930s must have carried out tailoring repairs for Fleetway Cleaners (Epsom) Ltd, for the 1936 Directory lists the building in their name.

Two years later his wife Emma, also a Tailor, is listed as the joint occupant. Fleetway Cleaners & Dyers survived up to the 1950s. For a brief period No. 8 was a Confectioner and Tobacconist business run by A. W. Jenn. Not long after this Harrington's expanded their premises by moving into No 8.

At No. 6 we find that John Shoolbred, Tailor and Outfitter, was the occupant. He had established his business there round about the 1880s. He was a Scotsman born 1823 and died 1902. His wife Mary who came from Devon continued running the shop until she died in 1913. Following her death the business became Shoolbred and Co. For many years Mr. Eric Wild owned and ran the shop. The shop finally closed around the 1970s and Gascoigne-Pees the Estate Agents moved in. Today it is still an Estate Agents by the name of Christies Residential formerly Domus Residential of North Street established in 1983.

William Dickinson Tailor c1905

Chings Basket Depot c1920s

Gascoigne-Pees c1950s

We are almost at the end of our journey up the North Side of the street and hope that you have not found the pervading smell of horse droppings too offensive and that ladies, the bottom of your skirts are not too soiled.

The 1905 Directory lists No. 4 as being occupied by Miss Betty Sarah Marks, Boot and Shoemaker, but by 1918 Leslie Ching, Basket Maker resides there. He remained there up until the outbreak of the Second World War. By the 1950s Gascoigne–Pees, the Estate Agents and Auctioneers, had taken up residence. They eventually moved to No. 6 as previously stated. The original No. 4 was demolished and the current building is the Princess Alice Hospice Charity Shop. A previous occupier was Bubbles Children's Wear.

The grand 'Tudor' building currently home to Peter Snell and Barton's Bookshop at the corner of North Street and Bridge Street has undergone a complete transformation over the years. Its postal address is No. 2 Bridge Street and its title is Bank Chambers.

National Provincial Bank c1950s

This grand 'old' house was built as recently as 1928. It is a fine reproduction and closely replicates the construction of a timber framed building. It was built for The National Provincial Bank and one suspects that the ship was not spoilt for 'a ha'pence of tar', and the result speaks for itself. The National Provincial Bank later joined forces with the Westminster Bank which was housed

Wild the Bakers just before demolition.

in the 'quadrant' building on the other corner of Bridge Street and so became part of the National Westminster Bank, now known as the Nat West. There is more to the building than just the external features, the rooms are decorated with fine wood paneling and ceiling beams complete the effect. There are those who say that it is a sham, which of course technically it is, but both the authors are fond of it, and so we suspect are many of our fellow townsfolk. For many years the building was

Bridge Street c1912.   *Bridge Street c1988.*

home to The Woolwich Building Society. Prior to 1928 this corner of the town looked very different.

The corner site, which also carried a Bridge Street address, was dominated by Wild the Baker whose business was housed in another quaint early 19th century building. Although it is rather sad, when we look back at the old photographs and see what has now gone forever, there can be no doubt, that like so many of their compatriots, these buildings were 'time expired'.

The building that stood on the site before 1928 was occupied by A.W. Wild the Baker. More information about his business can be found in the authors book 'Over the Bridge the Southern Side', published by the Leatherhead and District Local History Society. In this book the bridge referred to is the famous Kingston Road Railway Bridge.

We have now arrived at the end of our walk up the street but before we start back down the other side of the street we could not leave the crossroad area, without making reference to a long forgotten building that is beyond the memory of any living person. (Unless of course they were born in the 18th century!) Although Leatherhead still has a small Street Market, its claim to a traditional Town Market was established back in the 13th century, possibly c1280. There is mention of a shop in the market place and this was later referred to as 'The Stocks house'.

In 1673 John Aubry wrote that the market "hath been discontinued now about an hundred yeares. The market house was remaining here within these fifty yeares." From these observations

The Stocks House, taken from a Hassell water colour.

we are to surmise that the established market was in being for around three hundred years.

The building itself is rather mysterious and very little is known about it. However a map of 1793 by Gwilt, the County Surveyor, shows the building at the centre of the crossroads. It is thought that the position of the building caused the 'staggered' effect of the town's crossroads.

The drawing is by Hassell and might be relied upon to be a fair likeness. The South Side in sunlight, depending on the time of day, would seem to suggest that the front of the building is facing towards Church Street and that the buildings in the background might be located on the West Side of North Street. The town stocks for the wayward citizens can be seen in the front of the building, and the 'lock up', with bars on the window is to the side.

We have now reached the end of our journey up the North Side of Bridge Street.

In Chapter 6, having walked back down to the river, we will commence our walk back up the South Side of Bridge Street.

Chapter 6

THE SOUTH SIDE FROM MINCHIN CLOSE TO THE CROSSROADS

Standing by the site of the mill today we are confronted with a view that would have been unrecognisable some fifty years ago. In the place of the mill buildings Minchin Close winds its way up the hill from the river's edge. The following pictures show how the building of the flats, called Bridge Court, has transformed the bottom of the street.

Bridge Court   c2014

The photograph ('Wycliffe') shows No. 53, the ivy clad building. It was originally a private house, by the early 1920s it was occupied by Nevill S. King M.R.C.V.S Veterinary Surgeon, who remained there for many years. One of the authors remembers his Dad taking the ageing family cocker spaniel called 'Bonzo' to be 'put down' by Mr. King in the late 1940s. He cried his eyes out for days after. Who in the world today would call a dog by that

name? (Bonzo the Dog was a fictional cartoon character first created in 1922 by George Studdy. People soon adopted his name for their own dog.)

Mr. E. L. Caspari M.R.C.V.S took over the practice from him and remained there until the late 1960s when the building was demolished along with the cottages (Nos. 55 to 63) to build 'Bridge Court'. Photographs taken over 100 year ago show a magnolia tree, in the garden of the house. It is still there and blossoms every year.

Wycliffe c1948 - it is the ivy covered building in the centre of the picture. Note the old-fashioned lamp-post, possibly a converted gas lamp.

The bottom of Bridge Street c1910 - Behind the white posts in the foreground is the road leading down to the mill.

The picture to the left was taken c1910 and shows the fine group of houses that once stood on the site of Bridge Court.

In the 1930s through to the 1950s if you wanted to dress for the occasion look no further than George Stanley Clark, Furrier and Violette, (see advert next page) Modiste offering

Gowns to order, or own Materials made up on their premises at No. 51 Bridge Street. Their promise was West End Work at Moderate Charges.

Mr Clark remained at No. 51 well into the 1960s but we are not sure if he was in business or in residence. The Local Directories for 1984 to 1986 lists a firm called Eyes & Ears Ltd. CB Radio and Video Film Hire at No. 51. A good friend of one of the authors, Brian Chitty who was an electrician, also lived there. Also listed are the offices of a company still part of the Leatherhead scene to-day C. P. Daines Central Heating Engineers and Plumbers Cobham Road, Fetcham. No. 51 is home to Oliver Markham & Co Accountants today.

Very little is known about the early days of No. 47 and No. 49 because the rooms were listed as apartments. The Directories for 1910 until 1932 list No. 47 as Mrs Tanner, Apartments. In 1972 the Directory for that year shows the No. 49 premises to be occupied by D. Winter & Co Commission Agents / Licensed Betting Office. There have been many changes to both since then. Now at No. 51, we find Oliver Markham Accountants, who once occupied No. 49.

Today Calli's Corner, formally of Bookham, occupy the premises and offer Babies and Pets Ceramic Imprints, 2D Stone Impressions and 3D Castings of hands, feet and paws also Fingerprint, Hand, Footprint and Paw print jewellery.

We are now at No. 45. Before the days of the NHS and National Insurance many clubs and societies were formed to provide financial support in times of personal sickness and distress. Some examples include 'The Antediluvian Order of Buffaloes', 'The Ancient Order of Foresters' (there is still an active Court in Leatherhead), and of course 'The Manchester Unity of the Order of Oddfellows'. At one time all three Societies had

Possibly the Official Opening of the Oddfellows Hall c1930s
(Photograph courtesy of Mrs. Hazel Brown and Mrs. Eileen Pearce)

Courts or Lodges in the town.

The earliest mention the authors could find relating to the Duke of Connaught Lodge No. 6651 is in the 1910/1911 Directory of Leatherhead. It states that 'The Lodge' was affiliated to the Dorking District Branch of the 'Manchester Unity Independent Order of Oddfellows' and was established in 1885, for sick and funeral benefits. Meetings were held every fourth Thursday of the month at the Lodge Room, Duke's Head, High Street, Leatherhead. Secretary: Brother L.M. Wade.

The first reference to 'The Lodge' meeting in Bridge Street is recorded in the 1936 Kelly's Street Directory and that the building is their headquarters, Thomas Faux is the Secretary. It also states that the rooms above the main hall were occupied by Louis Hawkins, Plummer. The same Louis Hawkins went on to found Tower Electrics with Bert Swetman in North Street in the late 1940s. You will have to read 'Over the Bridge the Southern Side' to appreciate the Tower Electrics venture.

Have you made Provision against Sickness & Death ?

If not
Join
The
" Duke of Connaught " Lodge
held at
THE ODDFELLOWS' HALL
45 BRIDGE STREET, LEATHERHEAD

You may contribute for 10/-, 12/-, 14/-, 16 - or 20 - per week in sickness, with £10, £12, £14, £16 or £20 at death

Sample Table

Age last Birthday	Contributions	BENEFITS
16 to 17	2 0 per month	
18 to 20	2 1 per month	
21 to 22	2 2 per month	
23	2 3 per month	12 - per week for 26 weeks
24 to 25	2 4 per month	6 - per week for remainder
26 to 27	2 5 per month	of illness
28	2 6 per month	£12 at death
29	2 7 per month	£6 at Wife's death
30	2 8 per month	
31 to 32	2 9 per month	
33	2 10 per month	
34 to 35	2 11 per month	

Members accepted up to age 50

For further Particulars apply at :—
The Hall, 45 Bridge Street, Leatherhead
or to :—
Mr. T. Faux, Mark Oak Cottage, Fetcham
Leatherhead

A 1930s Subscription List.

Mr. Hawkins was a respected member of the Duke of Connaught Lodge and it is with grateful thanks to his daughters Hazel and Eileen that we are able to show the photograph that we believe to be the opening of the Oddfellows Hall.

*Thomas Powell's Blazer Badge
c1950s*

The late brother of one of the authors was a member of the Order, and he still retains his blazer badge as a keepsake. At the time of writing this article the Secretary is Mrs. Shirley Weight. The Oddfellows is a not-for-profit Friendly Society that relies on the good will of members and volunteers to deliver services.

We wonder just what the members from bygone days would think if they knew just what the premises were being used for today.

'Funky Fusion Belly Dance Classes, using a number of different dance styles such as Bollywood, Flamenco, Street Dance, fused with Traditional Middle Eastern Belly Dance, every Thursday evening at 6pm and 7pm'. Watching the participants would certainly make their hearts beat a little faster.

No. 43 has seen a wide variety of residents. The sisters Misses Mary and Blanche Hewlins arrived at No. 43 by a rather convoluted route. They had run three small private schools over a considerable number of years. The 1899 Kelly's Directory informs us that a school for Young Ladies was situated at Oxford House No. 4 Lower Terrace, Bridge Street. The school remained there until 1907, when it moved to Woodcote in the Crescent. The move was not a successful one and in 1915 the sisters moved back to Bridge Street, this time to Dudley House No. 43. The school by then catered for boys and girls aged from five to seven. According to the book 'Of Good Report', the story of the Leatherhead Schools by Linda Heath, the school closed in 1933. However, the school is still recorded in the 1934 to 1940 Street Directories as being at No. 34. We think 'Kelly's were never informed of the change in occupancy. The school may have been called Dudley House School but it was more affectionately known as 'Miss Hewlins School'.

In the mid-1960s No. 43 is called Holmes House, with Delahaye Holmes Estate Agents, Halifax Building Society (Agency), Hobson & Co Solicitors, and Leatherhead Staff Bureau on the Ground Floor. On the first floor was Herriot Associates Ltd., Insurance Brokers, Mid Surrey Mortgage & Insurance Brokers, Delahaye & Co (Leatherhead) Ltd., Building Contractors. The top floor was occupied by Dark & Bissell, Chartered Quantity Surveyors, D. Winter & Co., Commission Agents / Licensed Betting Office, The Independent Order of Foresters (Leatherhead Office) and SCC Educational Committee Youth Service District Office.

What a vast change since the days of the school.

Various businesses have come and gone since then, to name just two occupants, Attwood Insurance Brokers and Industrial Air Systems. Even the House has been renamed, it is now called Phoenix House and the name plate reads On Line Medical Reports Ltd.

The 1925 Street Directory lists Alexander Guthrie as being at No. 41, but no occupation is given. The same goes for a J.M. Walsh who was there several years later. Finally in 1936 William Ellis who was a Grocer is in occupancy, followed in 1940 by Duval's Ladies Hairdresser and ten years hence by Beatrice Ford Ladies Hairdresser. By the late 60s and early 70s there is a complete contrast in business use when Leatherhead Do It Yourself run by Bryan Strudwick is there. Shortly after in 1972 The Lighting Shop took over.

Today it is home to Cosy Flooring Ltd, providing floor and wall covering services. Prior to this Mount Green Housing Association were there, before moving to Bridge House (No. 33).

We now arrive at No. 39 and within its walls we will soon make a trip to the Orient. The 1925 Street Directory indicates a Grimley Harry Kimberley being there, but no occupation is given. He could be a relation to K.E. Kimberley who owned 'Kims' Garage in Church Road. In 1932 A. Primrose is the occupant. It is not until 1936 that No. 39 is recorded as an eating establishment. Erica's Refreshment Rooms, Mrs Gladys Ericson being the proprietor. She remained there for some time into the 1940s. In the late 40s and into the mid to late 50s it became the Blue Rabbit Cafe.

In the late 1950s or early 1960s, much to many people's amazement it became a Chinese Restaurant called the Kum Hong. One of the authors worked near London's China Town in the mid 1950s and was well aware of Chinese cuisine. The owner was a lovely man and his favourite saying was "You come see my kitchen – Spotless." After climbing up a couple of steps, both authors can vouch for this. The house special was 'Fried Noodles with an Egg on top' price Two Shillings and Sixpence. Another good thing was that the restaurant took 'Luncheon Vouchers'. The Kum Hong lasted into the 1970s. Today the Lantern House offering Take-a-way Chinese Food, occupies the premises.

KUM HONG
CHINESE RESTAURANT

Have a night out   ·   A new experience

- Business Luncheon served 12 noon to 2.30 p.m.
- 4 Course Chinese or English Dishes
- Menu changed Daily
- We accept Luncheon Vouchers

39 BRIDGE STREET   ·   Leatherhead

In 1955 John Hack's Company started the Luncheon Vouchers scheme. By the 1960s many workers were enjoying the benefits of the scheme whereby employers issued staff with vouchers that could be exchanged for lunch in Cafes and Restaurants, those who signed up to the scheme displayed signs that they accepted the LV's as they were more commonly known.

Arthur Phillips Grocer resided at No. 41 from the late 1880s until sometime after World War One. He advertised as 'Agents for the European Wine Company' also Whitbread's Ales & Stouts in Screwed Top Bottles, Earthenware and Glass of all descriptions, Articles of Best Quality at Lowest Prices. To-day we take Australian wines for granted but as far back as Victorian times he was selling Australian wine imported by The Emu Wine Company, which began life in London in 1862 and soon the famous Emu trade mark became the sign of premium Australian wines in Europe.

He was followed by Yardley's Stores. One of the authors remembers climbing up several steps and going into the shop in the late 1940s with his mother and recalls the wonderful aromas that those old fashioned grocery shops had to offer, tea would be sold direct from the wooden tea chests, along with dried fruit sold in blue bags. Biscuits would be sold from the tin and placed in brown paper bags (not forgetting to put aside the broken ones). Butter and the various cheeses on sale would be patted or cut to order with the lethal cheese wire and wrapped in greaseproof paper. Little did he realise that in the near future he would be doing many of these tasks when he worked as a grocer's boy for

Phillips the Grocer c1905

Yardley's Stores c1950

Bridge Street in the late 1940s showing The New Bridge Restaurant on the left and Yardley's the Grocer and the Blue Rabbit Cafe on the right.

Frank Butt Grocer and Provisions on the Kingston Road.

Yardley's remained in business into the early 1960s. At around this time Mr. Walter (Wally) Harper opened a Gent's Hairdressers at No. 35a Bridge Street but soon moved into No. 37 when it became vacant and became an institution in the Town. However, at the time of writing this book, the shop is closed and maybe the end of an era is in sight. Mr. Harper was ably assisted by his son Graham for many years. Part of the shop even became a Male Boutique for a period of time. An added attraction was the young ladies they employed. You would often hear, "you're next" but the customer would say "no I'm waiting for X" - No further comment. Once you had your hair cut you would go to the pay desk by the door, and more often than not you would be asked "Anything for the weekend Sir." We leave this to the reader's imagination.

Can you remember the days when fishmongers sold live eels? They would chop the head off there and then, wrap it up in paper and say "would you like the head for the cat?" Well this is what happened at No. 35. My, how times have changed.

Around 1905 Frank Bastable, Fishmonger and Poulterer is at No. 35. He remained there until the outbreak of World War One.

In 1915 James Oxborrow is listed as the owner, convenient because he lived at Bridge House, next door to the shop. The business continued under the name James Oxborrow & Sons up to 1943 when the sons Sydney and Ernest Oxborrow dissolved the business by mutual consent.

Ernest however, carried the business on alone, for a few

Frank Bastable, Fishmonger and Poulterer is on the right hand side of the picture. c1910

more years. One of the authors remembers it being a Fish and Chip shop and while his Mum or Dad waited for their fish to be freshly cooked, he could read the Marvel Comics, probably those left by the Canadian soldiers stationed in Leatherhead during the war. Other businesses that have occupied No. 35 include Bridge Sports, Squires Employment Agency, Spring Personnel, Tattooing and Piercing Services under various names; Carnival Tattoo, Tattoo U and Tony's Studio. Quality Solicitors, Palmers are now in residence.

This 1920s photograph shows on the right, Jack Oxborrow's fishmongers and next door the steps to Bridge House where he lived. Also, Phillips the Grocer with the white steps mentioned earlier.

In the 1950s and early 1960s, No. 35a was home to 'The Pottery' who offered Fine China and Glass to those who liked nice things. They were succeeded by Ludgate Travel Agency in the mid-1960s and by 1972 it is just called 'Travel' which was owned by Horsham Travel Agents. Today it is home to Levy & Friend, Art Dealers & Publishers.

In 1910 No. 33 was a Hairdressers run by William Suhr who later moved to the opposite side of Bridge Street at No. 22. The 1925 Street Directory shows the occupier of No. 33 as Bonner & Company, Boot Makers and No. 31 as Thomas Leavey Tailor. Obviously Thomas Leavey wanted to expand his business so when No. 31 became vacant he purchased it, before moving to Bridge Street.

Thomas James Leavey had set up in business as far back as the 1890s in Church Street employing three men. He was a well respected member of the community and also a Justice of the Peace. He died in 1928. The business continued in the family name for many years but was eventually acquired by Percy C. Turton, who in 1950 was living at No. 31. Prior to this in the early 1950s Mr. Turton had traded at No. 18 as P. C. Turton and Sons, Confectioners. Turton's remained in Bridge Street for many years before moving to Church Street. In the mid 1960s Nos. 29/33 is noted as Gents Outfitters and Ladies Wear.

Bridge Street in the 1920s
Thomas Leavey's shop is on the right hand side of the picture.

In the mid-1980s J. Grondona Consultancy Ltd (formerly Leatherhead Insurance Brokers) are at No. 33. In the 1960/70s John Grondona was a non-league footballer who spent much of his career at Walton & Hersham F.C. The business is still operational today at Albury Road, Walton on Thames, Surrey.

Mole Books Ltd was at No. 31 in the 1990s and offered a wide range of reading matter at special prices.

No. 33 now called Bridge House is home to Mount Green Housing Association.

A short while ago there was a fad for coloured oil lamps However if you were living in Leatherhead at the turn of the 20th century an oil lamp was a necessity and you would have no problem in purchasing one from A. B. Dearle Oil & Colour Man at No. 29 Bridge Street.

In the early 1920s Dearle's no longer existed and a Mrs. A. Day opened a Tobacconist & Confectionery shop. She was followed by a string of Confectioners, until the Street Directory for the 1940s lists the occupant as Jean Spidy, Sportswear.

However, later the shop offered a much wider range of apparel and a good selection of wools. The business remained for many years. In 1984 No. 29 is recorded as Travel Fayre Shoe Shop and by the 1990s Douglas & Co Estate Agents are there.

The 1899 Kelly's Street Directory for Leatherhead lists Thomas Hersey, at No. 27 Bridge Street. His main premises were in the High Street, Epsom but we have concentrated on the Leatherhead connection.

Thomas Hersey was born in Shere, Surrey in around 1858. The 1891 census records him living in Kingston Road, occupation Coach Smith. He married Ellen (Helen) Rogers (born 1860) in 1879. They had six children Thomas (1881-1958?); Mary Ann (1884-1944); William Henry (1888); Florence Hilda (1889-1956); Arthur Clifford (1891-1963); and Bessie Alice May (1894-1973). The late Victorian census shows that all the children were born in Leatherhead.

Mrs. Hersey lived on the Kingston Road, Leatherhead, however, something must have gone wrong in the Hersey household because in 1911 Mrs Hersey is living at Griffith Cottages, Epsom Common with Bessie, stating that she

Thomas Hersey's Shop is on the left c1910

had an 'allowance from her husband'. Thomas Hersey died in 1934. If you purchased a copy of 'Over The Bridge' you may recall that a reference was made to Mrs. Hersey's Tobacconist and Sweetshop in Kingston Road, no doubt she married into the family. Also, if you visit the Randall's Park Crematorium burial section, in the third row is a gravestone in memory of the Hersey family and some descendants of the family may still live in the area today.

For many years No. 23 was home to G.G. Newbury the Family Butcher, the records for 1924 to 1925 shows he had moved into No. 25 as well. But by 1927 he had also acquired No. 27. Business must have been very good indeed.

In the 1920s, William Day succeeded him at No. 23 and traded there until the 1930s. William was followed by Sidney Hawes, who was the occupant from the 1940s through to the early 1970s.

In 1936 No. 27 undergoes a complete change of direction when Raleigh Valet Service (G & A Goodrich) Dyers &

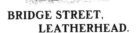

Cleaners, who had previously been in North Street, relocated there. They were there right up until the mid-1960s when the local Directory for 1967 states W.G. Holland & Co Florists are 'at your service'. They were previously located in North Street.

In the mid-1960s Lyes School of Motoring is listed at No. 27a but by 1972 it is in the hands of Percy Turton. Remember we first met Percy at Nos. 29/33.

For many years, next to the shop, there was a path that led to Leavey's Yard. Why was it called Leavey's Yard? The reason being, it was behind the shop of T. J. Leavey & Son, Tailors. Later to be known as Bonnett's Yard after W. H. Bonnett & Son, Blacksmiths who were there for over thirty years. L. J. Stone & Co Manufacturing Engineers succeeded them in the 1970s.

Prior to this in the 1920s, William Moses John Savell (late 12th Royal Lancers) set up as a Farrier and General Smith. Also, in the 1920s George Stemp Motor Cycle & Cycle Engineer had a lock-up there. In 1932 H. Warren Motor Cycle Dealer resides there. The 1940 Directory tells us it was home to the business of Alfred Croyden, Decorator, who had a lock up in the yard. To this day the yard still exists, as a car park, opposite the Five Rivers Indian Restaurant.

In 1924 No. 19 Bridge Street is a bakery owned by Cecil Whitehead. He was not there very long because a year later the Street Directory shows us that it is occupied jointly by George Stemp, Cycle Repairer who we mentioned above and Miss Louisa Brabazon, Second-hand Clothes Dealer. In the 1932 directory Miss Brabazon is listed as the sole occupant.

In 'Over the Bridge' a mention is made of Griffin's Shoe Repairers shop in Kingston Road, but in the 1920s Mr. Arthur Griffin also had a shop at No. 19 Bridge Street. He was originally at No. 9. In the 1930s Mr. Wilfred Harding carried on from him. One of the authors can remember Mr. Harding and the shop very well indeed.

No. 9 Bridge Street - Arthur Griffin's Boot Makers Shop.

Like Mr. Griffin he was a real gentleman, so caring to his customers.

In recent years some confusion arises because Nos. 29 to 15 have undergone several changes. However, some have retained their old numbers.

For several years the Queen Elizabeth's Foundation had a Gift and Coffee House at No. 19. It was a favourite with local residents and visitors alike; today they are located in Church Street, where they deal in second-hand furniture and bric-a-bac etc. Today No. 19 is home to Patricia Morgan, Optician.

Very little can be found about the early businesses at No. 17. However, from the 1920s it is well documented, firstly Mrs. R. Underwood Draper followed by Contessa Ladies Wear right up until the 1990s, when Contessa's moved to No. 11.

Bridge Street, Leatherhead.

This c1905 picture shows Hewlin's the Chemist and Stationers and the Old Leather House on the left. You can just see the corner of Wild the Bakers (on the extreme right) mentioned in 'Over the Bridge the Southern Side' with Shoolbred's Outfitters on the right.

Several businesses in Bridge Street can trace their history back to Victorian times, but Lloyds would be even earlier. Firstly with the Ragge family who might have been in business in the town, as far back as the 17th century. They were Saddlers and Collar-makers, making the leather rolls stuffed with rope which hung round the necks of draught horses, enabling them to pull great weights. In 1802 Robert Ragge proprietor of the Bridge Street Saddlery died leaving his thirty-six year old wife Elizabeth and three very young children. Within little more than a year she married one John Lloyd, a young man of twenty-three. They had three daughters and one son.

Little is known about him, just where did he come from and how did they meet? His background is purely speculative, maybe he was ex army, possibly involved with horses. Nowhere is he described as a Collar-maker, yet he carried on the tradition until his death in 1840, when his son also named John inherited the business. He and his wife Mary had two sons John and Alfred,

Mr. Lloyd and the old leather shop c1890 – The passage beside the shop led to a rope walk where ropes were made and stretched out along the walk.

and two daughters, Emily and Elizabeth.

It seems John succeeded his father during the second half of the 19th century and was himself succeeded by his brother Alfred. Both John and Alfred died in 1891 aged 51 and 48 respectively. Emily, the eldest of the girls, had married Augustus Walker a Mason in 1858. She then took charge and was assisted by her daughter Emily. Miss Emily carried on in the old house after her mother's death, but in 1905 she moved to No. 13 the next house down the street. From there she sold ready-made leather goods and remained in business until the mid-1930s. She died in May 1951 at the age of ninety-three.

JOHN LLOYD,

Saddler & Harness Maker,

LETHERHEAD & GREAT BOOKHAM.

Carriage, Gig and other Harness warranted of the best Material & Workmanship.

Established in the above building for 200 Years.

From the Epsom Handbook c1860.

In the 1920s No. 15 became a Tobacconist, a trade that would continue up to the 1950s. The first occupant was S. C. Bayley & Co., who by the 1930s would take up premises in the High Street. The shop was then taken over around 1932 by Hulme & Co Tobacconist & Confectioner and it was named 'The Cigar Box', for awhile it was also a Lending Library. Hulme & Co. had two branches, the one in Bridge Street ceased business around the 1950/1960s, but the 'Corner House' branch at the top of the High Street continued for many years after.

The "Corner House"   The "Cigar Box"
High Street   Bridge Street

HULME & CO.

Confectioners and Tobacconists (Whole-sale and Retail) - -

LEATHERHEAD

[Phone 596]

Motor Coach Agents—Bookings to All Parts

The Street Directory for 1967 lists Bernard Donner Optician at No. 15. Five years later Old Things Antiques are listed and in the 1980s the Directory lists it as Bridger's Estate Agents. Today Chewton Rose Estate Agents occupy Nos. 15-17.

When Miss Emily Walker ceased business in the mid 1930s at No. 13, the shop from about 1936 became Taylor's Cycle Dealers who stayed there into the late 1940s before moving to North Street and many people may remember them after they had moved to the High Street.

CYCLE SPECIALISTS

Main Agents for
B.S.A.   Raleigh
Humber   Royal Enfield
Rudge Whitworth
etc.

TAYLOR'S

13 BRIDGE ST.,

Phone: 431   LEATHERHEAD

Their departure saw the arrival of the Sky High Cafe/ Restaurant run by Syd Palmer. Mr. Palmer also had a business at No. 26 Bridge Street called the Sky High Catering House and the Chuck Wagon at No. 22a (see the North Side of Bridge Street). If you were a teenager in the 50s and 60s in Leatherhead, depending on your life style, you either frequented the Sky High or The Parrott Cafe in North Street. A friend remembers his favourite meal from the 1950s was spam fritters and chips, we were easily pleased back 'in the good old days'. Another friend seems to remember an aeroplane propeller being hung on the wall. One must assume that was the reason for the cafe being called the 'Sky High'. Can anyone else remember it? Mr. Palmer had two sons who were also involved in the business. His son John was an acquaintance of one the authors.

For a short while in the early 1970s Nell Gwynn House Jewellers occupy the premises, followed later by Bianca Jewellers. For some time now the Botan Kebab Take-a-way have been in residence.

We cannot find any references to No. 11 being occupied for retail use. One might assume that it was let for residential purposes only.

In the 1925 directory it states that Arthur Griffin, Shoe Repairer is at No. 9 before his move to No. 19. Directories for the 1930s period list Doretta Art Needlework Silks and Wools in the shop. The proprietor was Doris M. Pym, who also ran the Leatherhead Domestic Agency from this property.

Before the end of the 18th century No. 7 was occupied by the London Central Meat Company and they were there up to 1932. They were famous for their Canterbury Lamb. From then on it would appear to be a private residence for no businesses are listed in any further Directories.

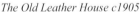

The Old Leather House c1905

The same scene c1950s

The Old Leather House was demolished by the Civil Defence in an exercise in 1939. It was not until well after World War Two that it was finally agreed to build three shops on the old Leather House site, namely Nos. 11, 9 and 7 Bridge Street with parking facilities in front of the shops. Back then the spaces would have no doubt been sufficient, how times change.

In the days before many people could afford a domestic washing machine they had to make do with a Laundrette. So when No. 11 became available the Bendix Laundrette came to Leatherhead. In the 1970s it remained the same facility but was now called Washeteria (Frigidaire). In the 1990s Contessa's Ladies Fashion moved from No. 17 into the more spacious premises at No. 11. Today it is a charity shop for The Children's Trust Tadworth.

From the 1960s to the 1980s No. 9 housed Smartahomes Ltd. Reference the advert below. How many older people can remember carrying home the large heavy wallpaper books containing the various patterns available? If not they would deliver them for you – now that's what you call service.

From the 1990s Kall Kwik Printing took over the residence and is still there to this day.

Early occupants of No. 7 were Foord's Furnishing Company whose Head Office was in Upper High Street, Epsom. For some reason one of the authors seems to think the Manager was a Mr. Bell and when Foord's decided to sell up, he took over and it became Bell's Furnishing Company. In the 1980s it became Kennedy Sports Ltd. The 1990s saw the name Herbert Sports above the door. Today it is the Los Amigos Café & Restaurant.

From the adverts that appeared in The Epsom Handbook for 1860 you can see that No. 5 had a long history as a Chemist. It all started with Edward Hewlins around the 1860s and was not only a Chemist, but offered other services, such as a Stationer and Bookseller. By 1905 William Richard Hewlins, Edward's son is in charge.

By the 1920s and early 1930s it is now Hewlins & Hughes. Both authors remember it as just Gordon Hughes who carried on the business from the mid-1930s until the late 60s early 70s when it then became known as The Bridge Pharmacy. A large 'gold' mortar and pestle was displayed over the front entrance. It is now in the care of Leatherhead Museum. In the 1980s No. 5 became known as The Carpet House, Carpet & Rug Retailers who spent many years there, before it later became a Coffee House. In 2015 the shop was totally refurbished for Nizam & Team Hairdresser for Men & Women who relocated from North Street.

Advertising in the Epsom Handbook c1860

In the 1890s Frederick Palmer & Son Watchmaker & Jeweller established himself at No. 3 until around the mid-1920s when F.C. Eldridge acquired the shop and carried on in the same profession and stayed in business

until the 1950s. Yet another Jeweller, S.G. Walker, was the occupant in the 1960s, but by the 1970s he had moved to premises in Church Street. By the 1970s the Anglia Building Society are listed at No. 3 helping you to save for a rainy day. They stayed there for several years before moving to North Street. It was also the offices of Durham & Co Solicitors, later Durham & Wilkinson. Today Huggins, Edwards & Sharpe Estate Agents are there.

At the turn of 19th century No. 1 Bridge Street was occupied by Miller's the Grocer, however, by 1909 Thomas Willey Cycle Maker had taken over. Soon the old No. 1 would be demolished along with some premises in Church Street. These changes can be seen in the following photographs. Thomas Willey relocated his business to London House on the corner of Church Street and The Crescent.

T H Willey's Shop is on the right c1910

London County & Westminster Bank c1914
This is another very fine building that suits its location admirably. We probably take this building for granted also.

The London & Westminster Bank was formed in 1834 and The Surrey, Kent and Sussex Banking Company were established in 1836 and soon had branches in places like Croydon, Brighton, Maidstone and Woolwich. It was renamed the London and County Banking Co. in 1839. By 1875 it had over 150 branches and was the largest British Bank. Later the two Banks merged, and The Leatherhead branch of London County & Westminster

64

Bank opened in its new premises about1913, having previously been in North Street from the 1870s. The London County was eventually dropped from the company name to just Westminster Bank and remained so until the merger with National Provincial in 1970.

We are now back at the crossroads and at the end of our journey. Apart from the changes that have taken place, in the buildings, businesses and the architecture, it is the complete lack of traffic in the older views, that attract our notice. The sounds and the smells that would accost our senses are difficult to comprehend. The smell of the oil lamps that would light the inside of the shops on those cold winter afternoons, mingling with the shops commodities, the smell of leather in the Boot and Saddle Makers, the aroma of the fats, sugar, grain from the Grocery Store and that memorable smell of fresh timber coming from an adjacent Carpenters workshop.

The tobacconist would no doubt do a fair trade in the sale of pipes, ranging from expensive briers for the 'posh' chaps, to the white clay variety for 'the labouring classes'. The smell of 'rubbed shag' would never be far away.

No doubt the Wet Fishmonger would also add to the variety of the airborne smells, not to mention the effect that the one or two horse power vehicles would contribute. Dare we mention it, but in a time when lack of access to instant hot water was the norm, the people themselves would contribute to the interesting ambiance. No doubt the ladies would wear a generous application of Lavender Water but her male counterpart, especially if he were a member of 'the labouring class', would in most instances, be wearing an application of good honest sweat.

It is worth repeating that 'today is tomorrow's history'. We are interested and take delight in finding out about our forbearers. In a hundred years time we ourselves will be the subject of curiosity and no doubt future members of The Leatherhead & District Local History will be saying to each other "how on earth did they cope?"

BIBLIOGRAPHY

Suggested reading to complement 'Over the Other Bridge'

Of course many books have been written about Leatherhead and the wider area of Surrey. The following titles are recommended reading and they have provided source information for the preparation of this book.

Over The Bridge - by Brian Hennegan 2009

Over The Bridge the Southern Side - by Brian Hennegan & Goff Powell 2011

The Inns and Public Houses of Leatherhead and District - by Goff Powell 2006

Leatherhead a History - by Edwina Vardey 1988 – Revised 2001

Archive Photographs Series – Leatherhead, compiled by Linda Heath 1996

Of Good Report – The Story of the Leatherhead Schools by Linda Heath 1986

Bookham & Fetcham – Archive Photographs, compiled by Linda Heath 1999

Leatherhead in Georgian Days by Linda Heath 2012

Leatherhead and District - Then and Now, compiled by Linda Heath and Peter Tarplee 2005

How Green Is Mole Valley: The History of Leatherhead Football Club 1886-2006 by Graham Mitchell and David Johnston 2006

Leatherhead Cricket Club: A History Over 150 years 1850 – 2000 together with Leatherhead Hockey Club (from 1985) by Patrick L Rennison 2000

Not all the above are L&DLHS publications – several are out of print, but may be found in Leatherhead Library.